# Between The Visions

To order additional copies, please contact us.
BookSurge, LLC
www.booksurge.com
1-866-308-6235
orders@booksurge.com
To contact author e-mail to: rayleneabbott@elitemail.org

# Between The Visions

## Seeing Through The Eyes Of An American Mystic

Raylene Abbott

2005

# Between The Visions

# TABLE OF CONTENTS

*Dedicated To Andreas.*

# PREFACE

St. Theresa of Avila lived in Spain and was born 1515 and died 1582. She is well known for her mystical states that took her into ecstatic experiences. Her writings of these experiences create the picture of God as her Beloved. "So sweet are the colloquies of which pass between the soul and God that if anyone thinks I am lying I beseech God, in his goodness, to give them the same experience" wrote St. Theresa of Avila.

Ananda Moi Ma was a well known saint of India. She too was well known for Divine intoxication. She remained for days without eating, sleeping, or growing tired as she communed with the Divine through ecstatic states of consciousness.

I am no saint, but I have had an inner longing for the Divine since childhood. This longing eventually brought me to my own ecstatic experiences and visions. At the pinnacle of my encounters with God, what I experienced is orgasmic ecstasy beyond my ability to put into words. The first time this took place, I was 24 years old; I was at a beach in California. *I lay down on the sand, when I became aware of the sound of the ocean waves entering my feet as a power that I had never experienced before. It rushed through my body with the primal force of a tidal wave. It traveled from my feet to the top of my head and straight on into space. Inner space and outer space blended into one, and I arrived at the source of all creation, the true nature of my Divine Self being revealed.*

Words are inadequate carriers of expression of the vast expansion that my consciousness experienced that day. The experience could be compared to an orgasm, except that the event was not restricted to any one location, but pulsated through all of my being. My mind had stopped. There was only God Presence.

This was the first step on my journey into the *knowing* that God exists. God is not a belief or a thought. God is not a mere concept taken from blind faith and parroted without living, inner proof, but is a tangible reality. This experience left me changed forever. And, it was only the beginning of many experiences I found through meditation and prayer.

# INTRODUCTION

This book has been written from the spirit of direct experience. The vision experiences are written in italics, which will make it clear to the reader when I am in the vision state. Many of the chapters I backed up with historical research material to lay a firm foundation for the visions that I am experiencing. Much of the confusion in religions during this day and age exists because for centuries we have been given only a part of the picture of true spiritual understanding. It is now time to destroy misconceptions around religion and spirituality. We can see in the world today how religious differences have caused wars and killing in the name of God. Religious differences have caused claims of being the chosen ones. This has been the great delusion that has kept the human race in the shackles of powers that want to control us. We exist in a time when the information revolution has exploded forth, revealing to us concealed secrets from many different religious paths.

There was a time when I would have been tortured or burned for speaking the truth of my own soul experience. This time is no more and I thank God/dess. May this book open the way and bring healing to both women and men. May we realize that we are Divine Beings in human disguise and may we learn compassion in the process of our awakening. May peace, truth and beauty restore the planet Earth.

# ACKNOWLEDGMENTS

I want to thank Andreas Mamet for opening the door of understanding to me and empowering me in ways beyond my own human conditioning. I appreciate his patience to work with this manuscript.

I also want to give thanks to my sister Linda Held for being there in the beginning of my own womb healings in 1989 and for sharing her own wisdom and experience.

I want to acknowledge my sisters of the order of the Magdalene, Elizabeth Kelly, Christy Salo and Sabina who have held and stabilized the energy of the Divine Feminine for several decades. May we all accomplish the Great Work.

CHAPTER I

# Giving Birth

I was living upstate New York in the small village of Accord. We had rented a barn that was converted into an artist loft. It was open, light and airy. It was a perfect place to have a home birth for my third child. The birth went well with two midwives, a girlfriend and of course my husband. After ten hours of labor the baby finally arrived. "It is a girl," the midwife exclaimed. Selene Joy was born on May 9th, 1982, on Mother's Day in a barn.

Birth is a very powerful experience and leaves a woman very open on many different levels. During the weeks of recovery I realized that this little baby before me was a great soul and had come to teach me.

This was how it all began one warm afternoon. Selene's cradle was placed close to me in the kitchen so I could watch her when I was preparing food. I was cleaning out the refrigerator when I came across a little vessel that looked somewhat like a plastic test tube, filled with mold. I put it under the faucet, cleaning it with fresh water, and I thought to myself, "This looks like some kind of birth control device." As the clear water washed through the tube, my baby daughter lay there in the cradle, cooing like a little dove. *Suddenly, the God Power began to surge inside of me with great force. My heart opened up like a woman opens herself to a man in the act of lovemaking. My heart opened wider and wider and I could feel the presence of God penetrate my heart, in the most complete feeling I had ever experienced.*

*God the Beloved took me, and I stood there at the kitchen sink in an orgasmic pleasure that satisfied my soul and body to the very last cell. The Power now moved from my heart and shot out the top of my head, and my spirit began to rise far above this earthly scene.*

*I realized that my daughter's spirit was guiding me, and even though she was incarnated into this little human form, her spirit was still very much one with God and had not fallen asleep in human consciousness. She took me to her, whom I call the White Mother, the Divine Mother—and whom some know as the Virgin Mary. There I experienced a mystical union with God that was pure and total, and was contained within the Divine Mother. I understood for the first time her many names: the Sealed Fountain, the Ivory Tower, the Enclosed Garden. She was totally united with the Beloved in ecstatic union, and this union she shared with me directly.*

My words cannot convey nor hold a candle to this experience, for it went beyond the world of thought. All sorrows and disappointments in my life melted in her presence. People who had hurt me—which more often than not had driven me inside—now seemed like *events* that took me into myself toward the search for the Divine. I could only feel gratitude for all the people I had known in my life, both the good and the bad, for in that moment I was home in the heart of the Mother, in complete union with everyone and everything.

This experience lasted for four days; I did not eat or sleep (but I could function in my family life). I would sit on the couch and put my finger in the air, and the whole universe seemed to revolve around it.

After my ascent to the White Mother, I began to descend to what I call—and now honor—the Black Mother, better known as the Black Madonna. This phase of the experience was not the ecstasy that I had felt in the higher planes; instead, it was hard work.

*My consciousness began to swim through the wombs of my mother, my grandmother, and the countless generations that had come down into the flesh. Genetic information about my family line and my children was easily read. It was as though I had taken a thread in a weaving, which was the outer-world picture, and pulled the string. All illusions fell away and I witnessed the one Spirit behind everything. This weaving of the outer "picture show" was made up of millions and millions of atoms vibrating, and even though it seemed solid, it was very lucid and ever changing. I could see the spirit of God clothed in the flesh of my children; their spirits were working through genetic patterns they inherited from mother and father, from grandmother and grandfather, patterns that had been passed down from each generation, generations that had fallen asleep to their spiritual birthright. The whole outer movie actually was a weaving of vibrating atoms, seemingly solid, but not. And I kept swimming deeper into the genetic womb until I returned to the first atom.*

This process lasted for days, and then, after many hours without sleep, I came crashing back to the earth-plane, not really wanting to return from the union that I had experienced.

It took me weeks to recover and years to totally integrate this experience into my life and to understand what it meant. At first, I only wanted the White Mother—the pure and the bliss—rejecting the Black Mother, but as time passed, I understood what this Black Madonna archetype meant to me. She was the mother-womb of the world, the ruler of sex, death, and childbirth. She was the embodiment of Mother Nature, and by not honoring her, nature was not honored, sex became degraded, and the Sacred was forgotten.

\*\*\*

After this experience, the Beloved became my secret garden and a spiritual haven within my soul. This was where I spiritually fed myself, where, even if the outer world looked like a desert, void of love, I could go to connect with my source and be spiritually nourished. Through meditation and prayer, I would find my silent Beloved who was always waiting for my return.

Now, this all sounds well and good for someone living in a monastery, living as a nun, but what about those of us who are in relationships in the world? How does one bring the inside outside? For, all I had experienced up to this point was my inner, secret garden, but I wasn't able to blend this into my male-female relationships. I knew I needed healing; my feminine and sexual self especially had a great need to incorporate the Divine. My Christian upbringing had left me spiritually split, not knowing how to incorporate my sexuality with my spirituality. Childhood sexual traumas had left me scarred and sexually wounded; I was filled with guilt and shame. I began to pray deeply for my feminine to be healed. I often prayed for this, for I would look at my daughter and want something better for her than the kind of pain I had suffered in some of my relationships. I made a vow to the Divine that if this prayer were to be granted, I would share my healing with other women.

This healing came to me in a way I never expected and never

dreamed could come true. But I am a witness to what has taken place, and I am here to share through the word with those who have ears to hear and hearts and wombs to heal.

CHAPTER 2

# Back to the Womb

In 1990 my friend Linda and I began work together with woman's groups as healers. I realized at that time how women allowed themselves to open up when men were not present. I found that many serious, sex-related issues could be dealt with and healed in the presence of the women's circle. An unspoken understanding and knowing existed among the sisters in our group, for it seemed everyone had lived through some type of abuse. The group consciousness worked together on "womb healing," and such issues as rape, incest, and sexual abuse were dealt with and healed through prayer, meditation, chanting and laying on of hands. A catharsis began to take place amongst the women: Suppressed emotions held in the body would rise, through the process of prayer and chanting would be released in a loving and supportive atmosphere. The vulnerability factor during this type of healing was of the utmost importance and required compassion and a delicate, gentle hand in order for the women to open up and release old wounds.

Because of the natural openness and gentleness they provided, I used flowers for the healings. One very powerful healing of this kind involved a group of about twenty women. The altar, made of a simple mound of earth, was decorated and adorned with the most beautiful-colored roses. We sang healing chants. As the group sang, the spiritual energy started to pour onto the women; at this point I disappeared and became like a hollow reed that the Spirit sang through. My hands began to tingle and I started to walk around the circle and touched the women. One woman began to cry, and in that moment I knew I was dealing with a deep wound. When the spiritual energy hits, you have to be ready for anything, because the body can shake uncontrollably and you may want to cry or scream, or just disappear into the silence. The woman who had been touched, began to shake and moan. Some of us went to her and laid hands on her to help her through the process. My hands touched her womb. Linda's hands touched her heart; and when a third woman's hands touched the suffering woman's throat, the silence of her pain was broken, as the agony that had been dormant in her body was unleashed. We learned that she had suffered an incest experience and had never revealed this before.

By this time the entire group was gathered around her, and we chanted. The body was shaking off the shackles of years of unspoken pain, and the voice was unleashed in cries of anguish. As she went through her process, we kept singing, even more powerfully, and the spiritual force was now showering from above, flooding the entire scene with grace. I went to the earthen altar and gathered many sweet-scented roses and began to place them upon her body. Her cries began to change and the pain began to ease, and gentleness came into her body. She began to go into an ecstatic state of bliss. We all kept adding roses to her body until she was entirely covered in flowers and all that remained in her was the sweetness of peace and the great presence of love.

✳✳✳

This period of time I spent working with this group of women was such an important time of learning for me, for I, too, was going through my own process of sexual healing. I realized that when a woman 's heart is closed, more often than not, her womb is also shut down, sexually. Unhealthy sexual relations register physically in the body as frozenness. The three centers in women where I found this frozenness were the throat, the heart, and the womb. When a woman had been told in a love relationship, "I don't want to hear what you have to say," her throat would be closed. The heart-center would be closed because of being hurt in love or because of not having been loved as a small child. And, when the heart was shut down, often I would see a woman's womb and sexual nature be closed. I also found that a woman's being sexually active did not necessarily mean that these centers were open. I found in myself and other women that excess weight gain around the hips was "unspoken padding" that said, "Don't touch me—I am hurt" (or, "I've been abused").

This is putting it simply, and sexual healing can be much more complicated, but these were keys to my seeing what a woman was experiencing in a particular moment.

I began to see that the era of the 1960s and '70s, with its sexual openness, created much sexual wounding that was just beginning to come to the surface in the '80s and '90s. I began to realize that the woman's womb is the vessel and that this open, receptive space receives whatever is emptied into it, and registers it in the body. Therefore, if a man is angry or violent in his nature, he deposits these negative emotions in the womb of his lover. The woman usually attracts this type of man from having an angry father or unresolved past lifetime karmas. Also, when one engages in sex that is devoid of love, this also becomes the message to the womb. Whatever the thoughts are during the lovemaking, they are registered in the woman's womb; like a tape recorder, the womb records messages into the flesh. These deposits can remain there for years, until the woman gets in touch with herself and begins to release them emotionally, physically, and spiritually. I found in my own process that often I had to *feel* the emotions that had been suppressed in order to release them fully from my womb. This became the catharsis in my own healing, and, as I got in touch with my own process, the group's healing was catalyzed, and vise versa.

***

At the apex of this process, I discovered that I had an ovarian tumor on my right ovary. The doctor who removed it told me it looked just like a man's fist! It happened that in too many of my relationships, I had chosen to be with men who carried unresolved anger. I saw that when this anger was directed toward me, I silently stored it in my ovary.

Symbolically speaking, the ovaries are the center of female

creativity. I was finished with having children by the time of my ovarian tumor, but I was beginning to become aware of my own creative process and projects. And, to truly be free in my creative process, I saw that I needed to release years of emotions that had suppressed my creativity.

The ovarian tumor was the culmination of years of unresolved hurt and anger. I had accepted male anger too many times, silently staying instead of leaving; there was also my own silent rage at being hurt and not heard. So, to begin healing, I deeply retreated inside myself and slowly began to deal with patterns both psychological and genetic as I recovered. I used prayer and reflection to probe into my past experiences and myself. Prayer was not enough for I found that I needed to understand myself psychologically also, so I put myself in touch with the old patterns that needed to be removed. And, once I found one of these patterns, I used various techniques, meditations, and prayers to help release what had been lodged in my body. The real healing had begun.

CHAPTER 3

# The Sacred Couples

Our women's circle continued together on our journey, healing both sexual and relationship issues. Linda's healing abilities were important to facilitate the group's healing. Her womb wisdom and psychological understanding were most valuable in my own healing.

Deep prayer and meditation in the woman's circle stimulated my clairvoyant abilities. I was given many visions during this time, but one vision in particular I want to convey, as it powerfully illuminates the male-female relationship of the future. Visions are an interesting phenomenon, for often it takes years before they come to fruition; it took seven years for this vision to manifest.

In the vision, I saw a new type of male-female relationship emerging on the planet. *Two columns of light, representing man and woman, stood side by side as equals. The male and female light-pillars were connected to their own Divine Self. The Divine Source poured through the couple as one pillar of light that then separated into male/female. The light went through the couple's bodies and deeply rooted itself into the Mother Earth. The Sacred Couples then turned toward each other and the light began to circulate through their bodies as one circle. It flowed from the crown of the male's head down through his chakras and entered into the base Chakra of the woman. The circle of light then flowed up through the woman's chakras and came out of her crown. Then it entered into the man's crown and down his chakras, making one continuous circle moving through the couple.*

*The couples then entered a huge ship that looked like an ark; they entered two by two. Hand in hand the couples were returning to God. An alchemy was taking place between the couples. A type of yoga was being performed that brought increased God Realization to each of them.*

I tried to apply this vision within my marriage, but it didn't seem to work. Even though some degree of spiritual understanding was present in my marriage, the alchemy for this vision to manifest was not present. Years went by before I could let go of my marriage and, by then, I had almost forgotten my own vision of the "sacred twos."

Our woman's circle wanted to go deeper into our healing and growth, so Linda and I got together and rented a chalet at a local hot springs spa. The workshop focused on dream work and on sharing openly with each other about our own sexual healing. The chalet had a hot tub, and a big kitchen where we could create herbal cosmetics and healthy food. To help release blocks in the physical, each woman was given an herbal body scrub, a flower facial, and a massage. Herbal bathing in the hot tub released tensions, which helped everyone to be relaxed within their personal process.

After the third day, we all were ready for a nature walk (taking advantage of my special expertise, which is reading the symbolic meaning written in nature). We hiked together as a group until we came to a clearing on a grassy hill. I asked that each woman find something in nature that spoke to her, a rock or flower, or a place that felt comfortable. And I asked that when they found their place, they become very receptive to what nature conveyed to them.

The women wandered off in different directions, and I headed up the hill to where a rock outcropping beckoned me. Two large rocks joined together in a *yoni* (vagina) shape. I jumped up on the rock yoni and straddled my feet on the two rocks that formed the vulva. Joining the rocks together was a clitoris-like rock. As I placed my foot upon the rock it moved freely and made a clapping sound that echoed through the valley. I began to create a drumbeat with the stone.

By this time, Linda had heard me rocking the clitoris stone back and forth, and wandered over to see what I was doing. We both stood on the rock yoni and power began to surge up from the Mother Earth. We had definitely found something! I rocked the clapping clitoris with the beat of my foot, and I began to have a vision.

*I saw Indian women come out of the hills from miles around, responding to the beat of the rocks. At the same time, the women in our group all heard my rock call and came together around the natural yoni shrine. They and the invisible Indian guests were now gathered together. One by one, each woman stood on the yoni stone and felt the power-surge come into her body. (It was easy to see how comfortable or uncomfortable each woman was with her body and with her power.) The rest of us cheered each woman on as she took her turn becoming empowered by this special place in nature.*

I had heard of maiden stones in both Native American and Celtic stories; many ancient European tribal societies also had fertility stones where women would gather to be empowered with womb wisdom. But this was the first time that I actually experienced such a place. It was an unexpected blessing for our woman's lodge, and the Native Grandmothers invisibly standing by were giving their approval.

CHAPTER 4

# Mirrors and Mountains

Working in women's circles gave me deep insight into myself. Other women became clear, reflecting mirrors of my inner female. This happened most vividly once in a gathering of ninety women at a Buddhist monastery. A large circle for sharing was formed, and everyone was given a chance to speak a small part of her story. A vision began to form in the middle of the circle as I listened to each woman

*I saw Mother Mary holding a rosary made of silver stars. As I looked deeper into the shining star prayer beads, I saw that they were mirrors. As the different women told their stories, I began to hear only one story; details would change but the same women's issues were being addressed. I heard only one voice, of woman struggling to become free and whole.*

Working with women helped me recognize abuse-induced emotions that prevented people from having healthy relationships. I saw many "womb issues" that manifested as weight gain—that extra padding that kept men at bay. These issues could manifest in physical symptoms such as chronic lower backaches and uterine or ovarian cysts or tumors. The worst-case manifestation having cancer of the uterus. However, one should understand this is not a hard and fast rule, for every individual has her own complexities that need to be examined. Environmental causes from exposure to toxic pollution also need to be taken into consideration when diagnosing physical symptoms. Unresolved guilt and shame can also register in the womb. The answers usually are not cut and dry, but as the healing process begins, layers of understanding begin to surface. Genetic history can play an important part in what has been inherited not only physically but also in mental attitudes passed down from mother to daughter. Realizing all of this, the only way one can get to the root of any problem is to deeply search into the history of one's family and one's sexual, emotional, and psychological background. And, last but not least, one must analyze past and present relationships.

I also saw the emotional damage that was left behind from abortion. I have no moral judgment against abortion, for it is a hard choice to make for any woman and it is her right to choose, but I do recognize that abortion can leave psychological and emotional damage that needs to be reckoned with. If a woman does not deeply look at herself during the process of abortion and clear the emotional issues—such as guilt or feelings of deep loss—problems can arise later down the road.

Symbolically speaking woman's bodies are the refection of the Mother Earth. When the Earth is not cared for properly, we can see this mirrored in women's lives, in a lack of support. I saw this reflection in the massive number of cases of women raising children with no child-support money. We can see this in the barren land that has lost its fertility through unnatural agriculture methods, strip mining, toxic waste—the list goes on. This lack of care and respect is reflected and lived out in the (relatively) small dramas and lives of women on the planet. Fertility clinics have now become a billion-dollar business. When the Earth loses her fertility through environmental waste, we see it reflected in scores of women who cannot have children.

The feminine side of God has not been honored and her sacredness had been forgotten. This has gone on for hundreds of years to the point that the very Earth herself and all that she lovingly gives has not been respected.

As the layers of womb healing peeled away through my process I began to understand I had to look at the other parts of myself and make peace with my European Christian ancestors. This came to me through a vision I had on Mt. Shasta in 1990. I was 38 years old. Mt. Shasta is known as a Sacred Mountain in Northern California. A beautiful 14000-foot volcano considered as the diamond of the Cascade Mountain Range. Also known as the Himalayas of the Western

Hemisphere. This area was the home of my Mother and Grandmothers; therefore I had deep ancestral roots connected to the mountain.

Battles were being waged over the fate of Mt. Shasta, between developers and environmentalists. The Native American people saw the mountain as their sacred shrine. Environmentalists viewed the mountain as a pristine place in nature worthy of preservation. The New Agers saw it as site for pilgrimage toward spiritual understanding. The developers saw it as virgin timber, money to be made, condominiums, and a ski resort. Everyone had his viewpoint. I had been away from the mountain (and the city of Mt. Shasta) for seven years—once it had been my home and sanctuary.

I was a member of a video crew there to film the mountain and conduct interviews with Native Americans and environmentalists about these issues. My job was doing the sound. (I was married at the time, and my husband was doing the videotaping.)

*The first night staying on the mountain, the mountain's trembling under my sleeping bag wakened me. I felt the earth really shake. I sat up, addressing the spirit of the Mountain, saying, "Wait a minute! I am here to help."* To say the least, I was scared.

The next morning the filming began and, to my surprise, I realized how many more people had been coming to Mt. Shasta than in my past. I witnessed the thoughtless trampling of the plants in the fragile meadow environments. "Spiritual graffiti" was strewn everywhere—medicine wheels constructed to the point that cement had been used so they could not be moved, sage sticks thrown like chewing gum wrappers. The spirit of the Mountain was not happy. This was a sacred place for the native tribes, and was visited once or twice a year as a pilgrimage. Even though I am sure the other visitors had good intentions, the scene was littered with spiritual trappings.

Well, to say the least, things had changed in seven years and the Mountain was feeling the effects. I went to a freshwater spring that I knew of and sat there noticing how many precious little plants had been trampled by the unconscious feet of fellow travelers. I felt the Earth cry. I began to meditate, and I slipped into a vision state.

*I saw four huge angels fly from the top of the Mountain to the little spring I was sitting with. The angels unfolded a huge sheet made of white light; each angel took a corner of the sheet and slowly lowered it into the Earth. Deep into the bosom of the Earth Mother the sheet lowered, then slowly returned to the surface of the ground, and on the sheet I saw the image of Christ. The image took on the form of the suffering Christ, much like that on the shroud of Turin. I heard the voice of Christ speak to me, and he said, "Mother, forgive them, for they do not know what they are doing." I realized he was speaking of the suffering of the Earth. The angels lowered the sheet again deep into the ground and slowly returned it to the surface. Again I saw the image of the suffering Jesus, and again he spoke. "When I was crucified, my blood fell upon the Mother Earth and she, too, became Christed, and now she is going through her own crucifixion." The angels lowered the white-light sheet for the final time and brought it up, with its face of Christ, and he said, "Go educate the people."*

This vision set my feet upon a new pathway, which went *back*—into the history and the understanding of Christianity. Why had Christianity become separate from nature? What were the resulting scars on Western civilization? How did sexual guilt and shame play out in a Christianity-based society? The keys to answering these questions were written down throughout history. It was time for me to find the answer.

CHAPTER 5

# The Feminine Face of God

My Christ vision on Mt. Shasta drove me into a historical search into Christianity. I had been raised Catholic, and as a child in the church's atmosphere, I learned deep devotion and discipline. I remember wanting to be a nun until I was about fourteen, when the world of the opposite sex kicked into my system. By age sixteen, I had left the Church because I could not live a teenager's sexual life and have God, too, under the Church's present structure. This was the beginning of the split I found in myself. The unconscious guilt and shame took years to overcome, years of understanding myself to become at peace with my own sexuality. One of the first childhood teachings I learned in Catholicism was that God is everywhere and in everything. (It was years later that I experienced this directly, in my ocean experience—my first encounter with God.) I began to question the contradictions: "If God is everywhere, God must be in the bedroom. If God is in everything, all of nature has the spirit of God in it. How can I heal these separations within myself?"

In 1992, at age 40, I had just recovered from my ovarian operation, which gave me weeks of rest, contemplation, and prayer. I was using the rosary throughout this time because of the gentle sweetness and peace that I found in this practice. Then, three girl friends separately—within a week's time—told me to get in touch with a woman named Elizabeth Kelly. I called her, but her answering machine message said she was away on a trip to southern France.

*A few days later, I had a dream of Elizabeth in which she was giving me a discourse on the Black Madonna. I woke up from my dream, the phone rang, and it was Elizabeth returning my phone call.*

I learned that she was a scholar of religious studies specializing in the life of Mary Magdalene. Her research had taken her to shrines all over the world to find the "feminine face of God." I made an appointment with her and, soon after, found myself at her home learning about the history of Christianity, a history I had not known existed.

Together we formed a prayer group of women that met twice a month to probe into the feminine mysteries of Gnosticism, the sacred marriage, and the many ancient Goddess cults that had blended into the present-day Catholic Church—things not known by most of the Church's followers.

"Gnosticism," from the Greek word for knowledge, was considered heresy during the medieval period. Gnostic doctrine recognized the feminine side of God, and referred to this as "Sophia" or the "Great Mother." The Gnostics' direct experience with the Divine was the ultimate conclusion. Through prayer, contemplation, and catharsis the Gnostics surrendered themselves into the Great Silence where all wisdom arose. I felt I was in the right group.

One of our first meetings was at Elizabeth's home. Her room had a large altar filled with fresh flowers, candles, and holy water from Lourdes, a picture of Mary Magdalene, and a statue of Mother Mary standing on a snake. The group of women sat in a semi-circle around the altar. We blessed one another with frankincense smoke and the Lourdes holy water. One of the women with a beautiful voice sang the Ave Maria, and a strong wind blew through the open window and seemed to encircle the entire group; it reminded me of the story of the Pentecost when the Holy Spirit came upon the disciples. We then said prayers and held hands, and once again I entered a vision state.

*I was staring at the statue of Mary standing on the serpent. All of a sudden, I saw her take the serpent from under her feet, straighten it into a staff, and hand it to Elizabeth. Mary whispered to me, "I am tired of having this under my feet."*

This vision was symbolic, and as the tangled facts of history began to unwind, I was given a greater understanding of what this vision meant.

The serpent symbology stretches across different cultures,

making its own twists and turns down through history. In India, the serpent is the Kundalini that lays dormant in the pelvis until it is awakened through yogic practices and rises up the spine and through the head, bringing the soul ultimate wisdom. With this awakening, great power is available, coupled with wisdom. Dogmas and doctrines fall away, for the seeker becomes the sought, and there is no more need for priests or religion—his is one of the many reasons orthodox religion veiled the truth.

Ancient goddess cultures referred to the serpent as the Goddess herself. The Egyptian queens carried the title "Serpent of the Nile," representing the Goddess in female form. Myths of sexual union between the serpent and the Goddess were told long before this was written about in the Bible. Serpents were worshipped also in Israel—remember the story of Moses making of his staff a fiery serpent: This story was telling of the awakening of his sexual energy, its rising as the Kundalini, which awakened his soul to great power and wisdom.

In the Gnostic myths, the serpent came to Eve offering her immortality and the knowledge to become God-like. Eve's eating the fruit of the Tree of Knowledge gave her the understanding of good and evil. So, not all Gnostic sects saw Eve as the downfall of humanity; some saw her, rather, as the messenger of the knowledge of immortality.

***

Now, more specifically about my vision of Mary freeing the serpent from under her feet. During the course of history, the Roman Catholic Church decided to include the doctrine of the Virgin Birth. (The word *almah*, written in the Hebrew gospels, was later translated as "virgin," but its meaning actually was "young woman." As the Church proselytized the pagans into the new religion, it incorporated some of the pagan beliefs and myths, and the births of many of the pagan gods had been virgin births. For example, the Roman war god Mars was born from the virgin goddess Juno, after she had eaten a white lily; in the biblical story of the Annunciation, the angel Gabriel came to the Virgin Mary holding a pure white lily and saying, " Hail thou that art highly favored. The Lord is with thee. Blessed art thou among women." So, we can see that the stories of the old gods and goddesses came bleeding through into Christianity.

However, in the old pagan religions, the feminine face of the Goddess was seen not just as The Virgin, but rather in her *three* aspects: the Virgin; the Maiden Lover and Child Bearer; and the Crone, the wise woman, or the hag. But, Mary the Mother of Jesus, through Church doctrine became simultaneously the Virgin *and* the Child Bearer—a role model that no earthly woman could live up to. Psychologically speaking, if a government, through religion, can control the *sexuality* of its people, it can control the people in general. Women, by being given the one religious archetype of the Virgin Goddess, are cut off from their own sexuality—although still feeling guilty and sinful—and thus the men do not achieve full sexual release.

I am not saying that sexual release is the key to men's becoming peaceful, but when sexual release is coupled with being truly loved, the "edges" seem to become much softer. When the average man is not made love to, sexual tensions and war-like behavior arise. It becomes easy to take that aggressive energy and direct it toward war and the conquering of other nations. And thus, Christianized Europe was born.

In Elizabeth's living room, the statue of Mary standing on the serpent was the feminine principal squashing her own sexuality. I saw that it was now time for all divisions between spirituality and sexuality to disappear, for spirituality and sexuality to become united within a new awareness.

CHAPTER 6

# The Many Names of Mother Mary

Elizabeth and I were on our way, in her Mercedes driving through central California to the small town of Thornton, in whose church a statue of the Virgin Mary of Fatima had been crying real tears. It was the seventy-fifth anniversary of the Fatima apparition in which the Virgin Mother had appeared to three children in the village of Fatima in Portugal. And this little Portuguese-American town of Thornton was having a major event.

We drove past a canal filled with blooming pond lilies; the canal seemed to go on for miles. The bright yellow flowers in full bloom were resting on the water, wide open to the California sunshine.

When we arrived at the small farming community, the celebration was in full progress. The church was buzzing with people, and a festival with booths selling food, beverages, and religious objects was in process outside. We decided to go into the church to pay our respects. A long line of people carrying flowers or candles was making its way up the aisle toward the main altar where the statue of the Virgin stood upon a large table. Many older woman were there, dressed in black and singing Ave Maria in Portuguese. Young women of Portuguese descent—some of the most beautiful young girls there—also made up the congregation. And Mary-devotees from all over the country were there.

Elizabeth and I made our way up to the altar of the Blessed Mother, lit our candles and placed them at her feet. We were going to leave at this point, but a saying of the rosary had begun, and the whole scene became like a freeze-dance; no one moved from her place until the entire rosary had been said. We happened to be right at the statue, kneeling and facing the main altar. The crowd closed in around us, the heat of the candles was intensifying, and the Hail Mary was being repeated over and over.

This was one of the most intense purifications I had ever experienced in a Catholic Church, and in that very moment I started my period. I began to break out in a profuse sweat. I couldn't even move. I just kneeled there praying, in sweat, blood, and tears. My body released an odor that "stunk to high heaven"; it seemed that the prayers were purifying me down to a cellular level. Could this be what Christ felt in the Garden of Gethsemane when he had prayed so hard that it was said he sweated blood? I don't know—and it didn't matter.

When the rosary ended, we left the church and the festival to find a motel, to shower and rest. We returned to the church around sunset. Outside were about forty statues of different saints resting on litters that could be carried, colorfully decorated with flowers and ribbons of every kind. People were saying prayers and rubbing candles on the saints, the candles to later light and burn at home. The statues were blessed, and they resonated with years of peoples' prayers and offerings. Each statue had become a living archetype for the saint's presence to come through and bless.

Being the historian that she is, Elizabeth began to speak of a time when the pagan gods and goddesses of Europe blended with many of the chosen saints of the time. This made it an easier transition for pagans to accept the new Christianity, for their familiar Gods—in disguise—are what composed many of the saints of the Church. For example, Saint Brigit's statue was there at the festival in Thornton, dressed in a nun's habit and holding a small image of a house; the *Celtic goddess* of hearth and home was also called Brigit.

The Celtic goddess Brigit dates back to a time long before Christianity arrived to the British Isles. The goddess had two sisters, and the three of them were often referred to as the Three Mothers or Three Blessed Ladies. Brigit's cult was centered at Kildare in Ireland; a sacred fire was laid in the temple, and it was always left burning.

Prayed to as the goddess of hearth and home, she was associated with fertility magic. *Saint* Brigit's feast day is, ironically, the same day as the pagan calendar's new year, February first.

The Church canonized Saint Brigit as the saint of hearth and home. One of the miracles she performed when prayed to was the multiplying of food supplies in the home. Her convent, associated with fertility magic, was in Kildare, where cows always had an abundant milk supply and shamrocks grew at all times of the year.

And the shamrock itself had been the symbol of the Triple Goddess long before it became Saint Patrick's symbol for the Father, the Son, and the Holy Spirit. Interestingly also is the fact that the sacred symbol for Aphrodite, the Greek goddess of love, was the white dove, which now is the Christian symbol of the Holy Spirit. Is this the hidden feminine aspect of the Holy Trinity?

***

Leaving Saint Brigit's statue, Elizabeth and I moved on to three other statues—of Saint Anne, the mother of the Virgin Mary; Mary Magdalene, beloved disciple of Jesus; and the Virgin Mary, the Mother of Jesus. Historically speaking, Saint Anne was quite an old woman when the miracle of Mary's birth came to her. Could the crone aspect of the ancient goddess be bleeding through this saint?

The Church often labeled Mary Magdalene as a prostitute, though the Bible never mentioned her name in association with the events when Christ was communicating with a prostitute—it was just assumed. Was the Magdalene the maiden aspect of the lost, Goddess trinity?

And, as the Church relates the virgin-aspect of the Mother, she is found standing on a crescent moon that is situated horizontally. Yet this horizontal-moon symbol actually is an ancient symbol of the Horned God consort of the Great Goddess. The crescent moon creates the shape of the horns of a bull lying on its side; in many ancient cultures, the bull symbolized the king and consort of the Goddess. In Greek mythology, Zeus was given the title the Bull; Egyptian Osiris, consort of Isis, was worshiped in the form of a bull.

Even today, the Hindu god Shiva, lord of yogis, is associated with a white bull. Shiva sits in meditation, with matted locks, and a crescent moon in his hair. Parvati is his female consort, and is often portrayed sitting at his left side. The bull represents male sexual potency and, now, traces of the male consorts of the Great Goddess are seen in Catholic Church statues, under the feet of Mary the Virgin as she stands on the crescent moon.

Saint Nicholas was also there among the pantheon of saints, giving his blessing to sailors at sea (Saint Nick or Santa Claus, as we know him today, actually is rooted in a much older, pagan deity known as Nickar, a sea god and king of the ocean sprites), to children, to brides, and to bankers. In his hand, he held three golden balls, which represented financial assistance in time of great need; this is the emblem of pawnbrokers today. He was said to live in the fourth century as the bishop of Myra in Lycia. One of the miracles credited to him was the supplying of three bags of gold to three sisters who were about to sell themselves in prostitution because they lacked money for dowries; thus, becoming the saint of brides.

\*\*\*

Elizabeth and I made our offerings and prayers to the various saints, and it dawned on me how many different aspects of Mother Mary there are: Our Lady of Guadalupe, Our Lady of Perpetual Help, Our Lady of Fatima, Our Lady of Sorrows, the Black Madonna—her titles were endless. Her aspects are many, covering different offices and offerings. I remember what an older, wise-woman had once said to me: "There is only one Mother of God but she has numerous aspects." Even greater than the pantheon of saints of the Orthodox Church was the number of more-ancient aspects of the Great Mother shining through in the disguise of the modern-day saints.

Darkness had arrived and candles were being distributed among the crowd, when out of the church doors came a litter carrying the statue of the Virgin into the crowded street. Hundreds of flickering candles lit the scene as Mary's figure moved through a sea of people and candle light, prayers on everyone's lips, and hope in their hearts that the Goddess still lives.

\*\*\*

After a good night's rest, Elizabeth and I were ready for a second dose of the festival activities. Moving through the crowd, we came upon a traditional May Pole dance. Young boys and girls in traditional, colorful costumes danced around the phallic pole, holding many-colored ribbons that were slowly and methodically woven around the pole. This dance had been a fertility ritual in old Europe. The phallic pole was inserted into the Earth to fertilize her womb and bring an abundance of crops and harvests. This phallic pole was even older than Europe's traditions; it was borrowed from the worship of the lingam and yoni principles of India.

\*\*\*

Elizabeth and I moved on through the celebration activities to find men cheering around a corral where a bullfight was taking place. This sport, which is popular in Spain, Portugal, and Mexico, is the last remnant of ancient sacrificial bull worship. Many older civilizations believed that their male gods could transform themselves into a bull. The Hindu Lord of Death, Yama, wore a bull's head; Shiva, at one point, became Nandi, the White Bull. There was the Israelites' Golden Calf, and Egypt's god Osiris became the Moon Bull. It was believed in some of the bull cults that the sacrifice of a bull and baptism in his blood would make a king a god.

\*\*\*

A parade was beginning, and Liz and I situated us in a spot favorable for viewing. The statues were carried on their litters, now decorated with fresh flowers, and ribbon banners with the name of the parish it represented. Before each statue walked the congregation's most beautiful young women, six girls for each parish church. They were fully decked out in expensive, white wedding gowns. Each parish had chosen a queen, who wore a sparkling tiara; over the white wedding gown each queen was clothed in a beautiful velvet cape that trailed behind her for about eight feet. These capes were highly decorated with Old World smocking, pearls, and gold or silver embroidery of crosses, doves, and the Eucharist or chalice. Each queen had a different-colored cape, and it was easy to see the time, money, and handwork that had gone into the costume of each participant.

Behind each queen walked two handmaids. They also wore decorated velvet capes, but in a smaller version. Walking behind them were the junior girls that dressed much like the older "royal party" but were in the ten-through-twelve-year-old age bracket. Many were holding rosaries and saying their rosary prayers; the church rosary group reciting the Hail Mary followed others. At the tail end of each congregation was its saint, carried on the litter.

You can imagine what this looked like, with forty different statues and one queen and five princesses in each group—it was quite the royal procession. I had never seen this before, and even having been raised Catholic, I never knew that this type of society existed within the Church's structure—for these were members of the Holy Ghost Society.

***

I learned about the Holy Ghost society a few weeks later when I visited a small museum in Bolinas, California, which featured an exhibit of the history of these Portuguese Holy Ghost Societies, including the crowns, the dresses, and the royal robes. I learned that the girls were chosen for their ability to understand their catechism and also for their charismatic beauty. Each girl went through a ceremony with the parish priest, who ordained her a vessel of the Holy Spirit.

I saw that this society and its procession was a modern-day example of the use of the Hindu Shakti energies, the power of the Divine Feminine. The patriarchal structure of fundamental Christianity has wiped out most of the traces of the use of this quality of spiritual energy. But when you dig deeper into history, you can see it shining through.

"Shakti" is a Sanskrit word that means "Cosmic Energy."

Tantric scriptures describe this as woman embodying the Goddess. Christian Gnostics saw it as the "Sophia," which is also referred to as "wisdom" in Proverbs in the Bible. The Gnostics' word "Shi'kina" represented the "spirit of glory"; the Jewish Cabalists saw it as "Shekina." Ancient teachings of Cabalists said that when God was in union with the Shekina, perfection was obtained. The Torah, or Law, symbolized the garment of the Shekina.

If you look at the stories of deities and of human masters, you can easily see the spiritual feminine energy at play. Jesus had his beloved Mary Magdalene. Saint Francis had inspiration from Saint Clare. In Hinduism, Shiva's consort was Parvati, and Krishna had a deep love for Radha. The Songs of Solomon reflect the great love of Solomon and Bath Sheba. When Buddha was seeking enlightenment under the bodhi tree and his ascetic practice of fasting was leaving him very weak, in that moment he renounced his old structure of renunciation itself. It may be worth noting that upon allowing feminine support, in the form of a woman offering him food, he became enlightened.

Even in the mundane world, this feminine energy is recognized. For example, when one says, "Behind every successful man there is a woman." The counsel of a wise woman combined with love and that right companionship can provide the power to move the world. Unfortunately, too many times, the wise, feminine energy has not been recognized, and when it isn't, we can see the negative effects on society.

And, when it *is* recognized, we can see the positive effects. The Iroquois Nation understood this principal when they formed their confederation. Several tribes were continually warring, and, after much suffering, they choose to make peace. They appointed the clan mothers to choose the chiefs of each tribe. They felt that the women's council would choose wisely because they were more apt to choose a chief that could keep the peace, as woman were more likely to value the preserving of home and family. The clan mothers were given the power to elect and dismiss the chief if he wasn't doing his job correctly.

In formulating the American Constitution, the founding fathers of the United States borrowed many of the ideals from the Iroquois Confederation. But they did not use "clan mothers" to assist.

When government is without feminine influence, we may witness more war and less caring for the people. And religion without the feminine can be more judgmental, following the god's law without love and forgiveness. And, more personally, when the feminine energy is absent in men, they are unable to incorporate the gentler side of themselves into their lives. Mothers can teach this feminine strength and love to their male children, wives to their mates, and female leaders—clan mothers—to male governing leaders.

For, when the Feminine is not respected, we see Mother Earth used without consideration for the generations to come. Sex is degraded and devoid of love. Mothers, sisters, daughters, and wives are not respected. The wounds resulting from this are found in our environment, our relationships, our religion, and our government. It is not a matter of feminine versus masculine but, rather, a matter of a balance between the two.

❈❈❈

During this phase of my journey toward the feminine face of God, I visited many churches, researched Christianity's history and symbolism, and continued my visionary experiences. I visited a local Catholic church, dropping in to pray during my lunch hour. Interestingly enough, the interior architecture of the church was exactly the same as that of my childhood parish church. Researching sacred architecture, I found that the arch-shaped elements often found in cathedrals had an arcane meaning, being the symbol of the Great Mother's womb. And as I was kneeling in the church one day, I noticed a huge arch that was the opening to the altar; on each side of this arch was a rose window, giving an ovarian structure to the church.

Rose windows have long been symbols of the Virgin Mary; Mary had innumerable titles with the word "rose" in them, such as Mystical Rose, Queen of the Holy Rose Garden, and the Rose Garland. It is interesting to note that in India, one of the titles of the Great Mother was Holy Rose; the temple was symbolic of her body.

*As I contemplated the arch and the rose-window ovaries, my eyes were drawn to the altar. My consciousness rose above the altar where the steeple connected to the church, and in a flash I realized that this steeple was the male principal, which was united with the Divine Feminine of the altar. The male-female union was actually secretly built within the structure of the church!*

My mind raced over other cultures that recreated this symbol in different ways. The Plains Indians had their medicine bundles which held the sacred pipes: The red stone of the pipe's bowl represented the mother earth, and its color was the blood of the tribe's ancestors; the hollowed pipe shaft was the male principal, and when these two sacred objects of the bowl and pipe stem were brought together, they represented union, which had power that could carry prayer to the Great Spirit, in the act of smoking. These pipes are so very sacred to the Native American tribes that they are considered one of the most powerful agents for communing with the Divine.

In the magical arts of pagan Europe, the mortar and pestle were tools used to make herbal medicine for healing. Healing prayers and incantations were said with the grinding of herbs. Looking at the symbolism inherent in these simple objects, we can see that the bowl represented the womb of the feminine, and the phallic pestle represented the male principal; joined together with prayer, they created sacred power.

India is a bit more obvious in its symbolism of the deities, with Shiva's lingam and Shakti's yoni representing the genitals of the god and goddess. This is seen in the lingam and yoni sculptures from ancient architecture to household shrines.

It is noteworthy that this sexual union refers to power and divine union, whereas in many religions, ascetic practices and the denial of one's sexuality is the preferred path to the Divine. In many patriarchal religious structures, the feminine aspect of God is totally denied, which leaves a lopsided, incomplete doctrine.

CHAPTER 7

# Forgiving the Inquisitor

My inner search into Christianity took me on a pilgrimage to Italy. I flew to Rome and stayed in a monastery, where I met fellow travelers who were on their way to Assisi to visit the shrine-sites of Saint Francis and to pray.

Being in Rome for the first time, I wanted to visit the sights, and one of the first stops was the courtyard of an old church. Even though the church was very beautiful inside, where I felt the real spirit was at the fountain outside in the courtyard. Covered in ivy, a small fountain with a statue of the Madonna and Child caught my eye. The sweetness of the sound of the water, the coolness of the ivy growing up the wall and clinging to the edges of the fountain, opened my heart to the spirit of the Mother in nature, in her utter simplicity. This was the place I said my first prayers for the journey I was about to embark on.

At the monastery, I shared a room with two women I became close to, and we became fellow travelers. One of our first stops was the Colosseum, which was a short walk from the monastery. On our way, we passed the temple of Vesta. I was told that a perpetual fire used always to burn there and that temple priestesses known as the vestal virgins kept it. They took vows never to marry, and also shaved their heads. They symbolically became the brides of Rome. The Roman Catholic convents, whose nuns took similar vows, becoming brides of Christ, borrowed this tradition.

Before we came to the Colosseum, we passed by the ruins of the housing for the lions and other animals that were used in the gladiators' games. We approached the Colosseum, and beyond the outer picture of tour buses and people of all kinds, I felt uneasy being in the atmosphere of this grand monument to ancient Rome. I thought—but more than thought—I *felt* the history. I *felt* what had taken place there. I felt the people who had died there for the sake of others' sadistic pleasures. I thought of the Christians that were martyred because of their faith in God. I could feel the blood that stained this place and time and that still was registered on an etheric level in the Colosseum's atmosphere. I walked away, glad to be out of there.

*****

My sensitivity to the land and places and what was registered in them had been developed and heightened by my years of training by Native American teachers. I had learned that whatever takes place becomes encoded into the environment and stays there until a person who embodies the spiritual office prays over the site, purifying it and ridding the land of the traces of transgressions of divine law. The reason certain places engender feelings of comfort or discomfort in us is that the sum of all historical actions remains as a living, psychic presence overlying the material environment. Thus, if one were to look at a given place with open, psychic perception, one would be surprised to find entirely *different* settings and events.

Consequently it is possible to find the same history repeating itself over and over again through war and grievances. The people in power may change, but the same events take place. It seems that souls who still have to learn the lessons of violence become attached to such places and play out their earthly dramas.

It is the same regarding positive vibrations that have been registered in the earth. Many of the European Christian shrines were once pagan shrines to the Goddess. Thousands and thousands of years of worship have been "placed" in the same spots. Of course, it was much easier to convert the pagans if their old shrines to the Goddess simply were given new names, of saints, or if they became churches, of the Blessed Mother. Nevertheless, the prayers were still registered in these sacred places. One of the most powerful things I experienced when visiting shrine sites was when I kneeled down to pray there. I felt all the prayers that people have said there before me, for hundreds of years, prayers that gave these places immense power. Many of these places became "time gates" to the Divine. When you visit and pray there, your prayers are answered swiftly, because the power of all those who prayed before is still registered in the same spot.

***

The next day, after mastering Rome's bus system, we took a trip to the Vatican. The bus was as crowded as a sardine can, but the warmth of the people and the subtle interactions between the Italian men and women amused me. When we had arrived at the Vatican, I stood outside St. Peter's awed by the grandeur of the pantheon of patriarchs that were erected on pedestals towering heavenward. We made our way into the halls of the Vatican, which held some of the greatest artworks that I had ever been exposed to. I had just entered into the halls of time and history, which were still alive and breathing in paintings, tapestries, stone, manuscripts, and sculptures.

A stone sculpture of Artemis, the many-breasted moon goddess, captured my attention. In the Artemis myth, she gave birth to all animals and her multiple breasts nursed the creatures she had created. She was called the Virgin Huntress. Some of her older cults sacrificed and beheaded men who came too near her temple. Artemis's temple daughters wore masks of dogs, and ritually chased the Horned God Actaeon. In this myth, Actaeon was torn into many pieces, and in many ancient barbaric tribes, this sacrificial death was played out in dramas of the sacred Stag King. It was said that if a man witnessed the goddess taking her ritual bath, he would be doomed to die. The sacrifice of the Stag King was believed to fertilize the earth.

This drama was also played out in the context of other ancient cultures and their mythological goddesses, in both the Mediterranean and the Middle East. The *hieros gamos,* or Sacred Marriage, was the joining together of the high priestess and sacred king. The queen always chose the king, and his virility was an important aspect because he was tied to the land by making love with the high priestess. The priestess became the embodiment of the Earth goddess, and the king would make love to and symbolically fertilize the Earth. On an unfortunate note, he was often sacrificed in order to ensure the resurrection of the next season's harvest. Some ancient goddess cults sacrificed yearly while others did so only when the queen lost her interest sexually for the king, or when the king lost his virility, which was thought to be important for the health of the land.

The savior-king sacrifices also occurred in the story of the Egyptian goddess Isis and her husband, Osiris, whom she resurrected into Horus. This story repeated itself in Babylon, ancient Ethiopia, Crete, Greece, and Assyria, and in Rome during the time of Caesar. Even in ancient Ireland, the kings were said to mate with Queen Mab, the fairy queen, and make love to the land. It was believed that if a king lost his queen, the kingdom would collapse—the royal male's loss of his Shakti energy bringing ruin to the land. You can see this, also, in the legend of King Arthur and Guinevere. And Jewish Cabalists believed that when the Creator had lost his Shekina, all manner of evil took place. The queens were the embodiments of the land, and the kings were the creators, fertilizing the earth.

❋❋❋

Moving through the Vatican, I had entered the hall of tapestries. They were exquisite, woven in rich colors embellished with golden threads. The life of Christ and Mary was portrayed in these extraordinary weavings. Many months prior to my visit, I had steeped myself in research of the flower lore and symbolism of medieval Europe. And, as flowers and nature were the backdrop of each setting in these tapestries, the symbolic meanings were speaking to me vibrantly. I could easily see the symbols of the ancient Goddess shining through the Christian motifs.

One such tapestry hung over the hall's doorway. Three bees were woven on a panel; this three-bees motif had been the symbol for resurrection in the ancient Goddess cults. The bee itself was symbolic of the Great Goddess. This bee symbol reflected the Goddess's fertility magic, and death and resurrection rites. The queen bee kills the drone after mating; bee myths assured that the Goddess restored life to her dead lover through the application of magic bee balm, giving the ancient kings the official name of the "Anointed One." Also, honey was one of the components of the liquid used in embalming the dead; honey cakes were ancient offerings on Aphrodite's altar.

The story of the sacrificial king was woven into the symbols in the tapestries hanging before me. The ancient mythos was bleeding through into the present day—Christ's story was becoming more obvious.

Flower symbolism also was woven within the threads, for example, the lily of the valley, which was called Our Lady's Tears. In ancient flower lore it meant happiness and the uplifting of the spirit. During medieval times and on into the Renaissance, many flowers that had been devoted to pagan goddesses became flowers of Mary; over six hundred plants during this time period were dedicated to her. These flowers often were addressed as "Our Lady." Our Lady's Mantle, *Alchemilla vulgaris*, was one of Mary's flowers, and it was one ingredients used by medieval alchemists to create the philosopher's stone. Lady's Bedstraw was used as Christ's bedding in handcrafted nativity scenes.

Painters and craftsmen used this flower symbolism in their artworks to tell the viewer the *hidden* meanings of their works. One of the tapestries I was admiring that day was filled with red roses, with Christ blessing a woman kneeling before him. His brilliant red robe and the red roses still held the color through the test of time. Roses have always been associated with the Virgin Mother, but before Christianity, they had been the badge of Venus, the sign of prostitutes in ancient Rome. Red roses represented the sexual mysteries of the Goddess, and white roses represented the aspect of her virginity. Christianity adopted these symbols, but the red rose became Mary's suffering and the white rose, her purity. As I stood in front of the rows of Vatican tapestries, I was filled with awe by the sight of all these flowers woven here among the deities.

\*\*\*

Today in some Catholic parishes, the crowning of Mary in the month of May is one of the most beautiful rituals still preserved. This ritual has deep roots, in Roman times, with the crowning of the goddess Flora, which was celebrated in May. We see this same custom in pagan Europe, crossing over as May Day, with the crowning of the May Queen and the dancing around the phallic May Pole. Interestingly enough, in even more ancient times, the rose wreath represented the Sacred Marriage and small chaplets of roses were placed around the lingam of the phallic god.

I stood looking at an elaborate white porcelain kneeler, which was covered in hand-painted flowers of every kind. At its center was a painting of the Assumption of Mary into heaven. I contemplated the importance of the aspect of the Blessed Mother Mary in religious history. When the patriarchal influence had finally taken over pagan Europe, Mary held the last remnants of the Great Goddess culture. Later, when Christianity went through the Reformation, the feminine aspect of God was totally stripped from Church doctrine. But, even through the fuller picture of the Goddess in all her aspects had been denied, she still lived and held a place in the hearts of many people. The loving mother goddess had not forgotten her children; her form had changed, but her presence lived on through the Blessed Mother Mary.

***

As I went deeper into the halls of the Vatican, I became painfully aware of the suffering of the martyrs of the Church, for this, too, was represented in artwork. I thought of all the Christian blood that had been spilled at the Colosseum by the hands of cruelty. When the pagan rulers were in power, the Christians were persecuted. But as the wheel of time turned and Europe became Christianized, the strong arm of the Inquisition burned and tortured thousands of people who were pagans or who spoke out against Church doctrine. The same bloody mistakes took place; the power structure had simply changed hands.

The Inquisition of the Catholic Church is its darkest point in history. The old religion's nature deities, such as Pan, took the form of the devil through Church propaganda (while pagan holidays became the church's holy days). Unspeakable tortures were perpetrated to force victims to confess to crimes never committed. Women, men, and young children were burned, condemned without mercy. This was not only a way to force a religion onto people that did not believe in its doctrine, but it was also very profitable. Condemned heretics would have their land and belongings taken away and divided up between Church and civil courts. The victims of the Inquisition and, later, of the Protestant witch hunts stretched out over five centuries. Those within the Church structure who spoke out against the Inquisition found themselves in the torture chambers and eventually were burned. Women were often raped and then their tongues cut out so that on the way to the burning stake, they could not speak of what had taken place. Entire towns of people were condemned and burned as witches or heretics. The atrocities and the suffering reminded me of what Christ had said: "Many shall suffer for my name's sake." I felt that he wasn't speaking only of the martyrs of the Church, but also of those who had died because of Church policy.

\*\*\*

My mind drifted back to memories from a few years before, when a particular statue came to me, of the Virgin Mother of Fatima. This statue had been blessed and then brought from Fatima in Portugal. It was the property of a woman's rosary group, and it traveled from home to home, bringing with it many people's prayers and blessings. When it came to me, I was astounded by the power that it held.

I set up an altar in my bedroom and placed her there. I only had her for twenty-four hours, and within that time frame, women started showing up at my home. One woman had breast cancer; another thought she had a brain tumor and was planning to go to the doctor to confirm this; and a third woman did have a tumor. People came to my bedroom, sat on the floor, and just began to weep in front of this blessed object. The healing and compassion that this sacred object emanated was profound. I felt it was a gateway through which the energies of the Divine Mother's presence funneled.

*I was sitting in front of the statue when I began to go into a visionary state. I started to see ashes raining down from heaven. So many ashes there were that the whole altar was covered and the Mother looked very saddened. I realized that these ashes were from all the souls that had been burned during the years of the Inquisition. I prayed for healing and understanding.* When the healing time with the statue of Fatima was over, I returned it to the rosary group.

Within days of this experience, I was invited by a friend to go to a pagan celebration for Halloween, or "Samhain Sabbat" in the Wiccan religion. "Wicca" is the remnant of the old pagan traditions. It is not some cult that worships the devil, but a group of people who honor the spirit of nature and who have developed the wisdom of the gods and goddesses of nature. The word "Wicca" comes from the Old English word "wic," which is the life force in the plant kingdom that rises and falls in the seasonal cycle; the holidays of the Wiccan are celebrated around nature's cycles. Samhain is one of the high holy days in the pagan calendar. Just as with all saints' days, the day after Halloween became a holy day in the Christian church. Samhain is the day of the dead, a time that one honors all those who are deceased— friends and relatives. It is a time when the veil between the worlds is thinnest. Those who have the gift of clairvoyance can communicate easily with the deceased. One's ancestors are honored and food is left to feed hungry souls on the other side.

This concept is not far outside my Catholic childhood upbringing. Many times my mother reminded me to light candles for those who were dead and to pray for their souls, especially for the relatives. This was how I was raised, and it left a strong, lasting impression.

Well, there I was, outside an old airplane hanger in San Francisco where the modern-day pagans had gathered for their annual celebration. We had to wait in a very long line, but finally we arrived at the celebration. Four altars were erected in the four corners of the building. Each altar represented one of the four natural elements: fire, earth, water, and air. People were going to the different altars, lighting candles and making prayers and offerings. Hundreds of people had gathered for this event. I counted more woman than men. A stage event was beginning, where the high priestess of the group invoked the Great Goddess and her Horned Consort. Actors on stilts came out, dressed as the Goddess and the Horned God, and walked through center stage. As she invoked each of the elements, the actors that played the parts danced through the crowd. It was a well-organized outer drama, but it was the inner realities I had come for.

I sat on the cold floor among a mass of people. I closed my eyes and began to meditate. My soul began to travel on the time-line continuum; this is a place that I sometimes go, where past, present, and future all exist together in one moment. It becomes easy to read the past lives of the souls that are before you. (Many religions believe in reincarnation, in the soul passing through many lives to ultimately gain the wisdom that is an eternal spark of the divine mind.)

So, here I am, reading the group soul before me, and this is what I saw. Imagine people gathering at a party, and how women oftentimes gather in little groups chit-chatting. This felt the same way, except that my perception took place on a deep, soul level.

*I saw one small group that I called the Salem girls. One young woman was dressed in black velvet with red and white striped socks and with silver-buckled, black shoes. If she'd worn one of those little white pilgrim caps, she would have looked like she'd just walked off the streets of Salem. The entire group surrounding her came from this period in history. Another group looked like the old European gypsies who were heavily persecuted during the burning times; the women looked like they carried crystal balls in their back pockets and could cross your palm and predict your future. Another group came straight out of Greece, and embedded in their souls, they carried the blueprints of knowledge of ancient Greece. With each group, I could see how their lives were cut down because of persecution. And they had once again reincarnated, picking up where they had left off.*

\*\*\*

The artworks deep in the Vatican reminded me also of my own soul's memory of being burned at the stake. This was something I had had to pass through again, in this lifetime, as I began to awaken in my consciousness.

I actually met, in this lifetime, the man who had been my inquisitor. Many of the circumstances from the past life played out again in this one, differently, but the same old story was attempted.

Even though I went through a lot of suffering with him, I managed to escape before becoming a total victim. I had such hate for this man that it took many years for me to forgive things that he had done. One day after being on the phone with him in another battle of the wills, a still, small voice inside said, "Are you going to go to the grave again hating him?" It was then that understanding began to dawn. I realized that I had cursed this being while I was burning on the stake and that the only reason I was connected to him in this life was because I had never forgiven him. This had kept me hooked into his soul. After realizing this, I actually prayed to forgive him, and I did this every day for eight months. At first, I didn't mean it, but after making it my practice, the hate actually gave way and forgiveness was established. When I saw him the next time, all the antagonistic feelings had dissipated. This man treated me in an extremely friendly way. I just sat quietly, never telling him what I knew or what I did. The power of forgiveness *is* magical.

This power of forgiveness is something that could benefit some of the pagan groups that I associated with, groups in whom I saw a soul memory of the burning times. I noticed some members were still holding anger and resentment for the injustices that had taken place. I believe that there comes a time when a soul must reconcile and find peace with those who took their life in a previous time. In my own experience, the only thing that had kept me hooked into my former inquisitor's soul was my own lack of forgiveness. Whatever seeds he sowed created his own karma, but I became free of him when I was able to release my anger from this lifetime and the lifetime before. He then disappeared out of my life and my own lesson was complete. Anger and resentment between two souls are like dark hooks that keep the souls entangled from one lifetime to the next until the lessons are learned and the souls become free. This does not excuse the events of historical karma, but it gives one a bigger picture of what took place and how to become free, in a karmic sense.

\*\*\*

Back in the Vatican I start to make way into the Sistine Chapel.

Over a loud speaker, a man asked the crowd to please be quiet and respectful, for we were in a sacred place. I made my way through the crowd and stood at the center of the chapel with my girlfriend Marlene. I pointed silently to the ceiling, and there it was, directly over us: Michelangelo's masterpiece painting of God's finger touching Adam's finger. We were at the center of creation.

I felt the need to go sit by myself, but to find a seat amongst all the tourists was a small miracle in itself. After a few minutes, a place at the back wall of the chapel cleared out, and I sat down on a cold, gray marble bench. My direct view was facing the main altar where hung a huge wooden Cross with Christ. Behind the Cross was Michelangelo's painting of Hell, purgatory, and then rising into Heaven where Christ, Mary, and the assembly of saints and angels gathered. My eyes were taken to the bottom of the painting and the impact of all the suffering of humanity down through time hit my soul dramatically through the artwork. The suffering Christ on the Cross just hung there, and I found myself uncontrollably weeping as I sat in this cold, dark little corner of the chapel. All the visions and events that I had witnessed while going through the halls of the Vatican made their full impact. *As I sat there crying, I heard Christ crying out to me on the Cross, "Get me out of here." I was shaken to the core of my being. I stood up, and as I walked out of the chapel with all its opulence, beauty and richness, I looked back at the crucified Christ through a wall divider made of wooden bars. As I stared back through the bars, looking back at the crucifix of Christ, I got the impression of prison bars, and that the spirit of the* true *Christ was imprisoned.*

\*\*\*

I continued down the corridors of the Vatican and stared into the glass display cases and saw elaborate, golden Eucharist holders, which are called monstrances. I looked down at the dates of these sacred objects and saw that they covered a time span from 1500 to 1600. A realization came to me, and I knew this was the gold that had been brought from the New World. I asked myself, "How many Native Americans died to bring this wealth back to Europe?" Again, a vision of Christ came into my mind's eye.

*I saw Jesus at the table of the Last Supper. Christ's own blood was running over the table, and then I saw the blood of the Christian martyrs. But it was not only the Christians' blood that stained this vision table, but also the blood of the martyrs of the Inquisition and the blood spilled in the genocide of the Native Americans. My vision was one bloody mess. Christ was crying out in agony because of the separation and the suffering.*

"Forgiveness" was in the last words that Christ spoke on the Cross. Christ's life was an example of mercy and forgiveness. It is this example we need to follow in order to forgive the actions of the past. There is no greater freedom than to be able to let go and forgive completely, and to give all of yourself and your enemies to God. The weight of hate, ignorance, and judgment has built walls around countries, cultures, religions, and races. We are all asked to come to Christ's table and partake of the Body of Christ. We all are a part of that Body. The spirit of Christ is beyond dogmas and doctrine, and never needs to be proved but is found only within each individual heart. Even though power structures were built around Christ's teachings, the word and the law often went against Christ's words. "Father, forgive them, for they know not what they do." The sacrifice has been great for Christ, for the martyred saints, for those on the burning stake, for the Native Americans whose blood was shed on the Earth of the New World. We *all* are the Body of Christ; may forgiveness flood the hearts that need forgiving and may forgiveness flow into the hearts that need to forgive. This and only this will free everyone from the generational sins of the past. The Church has been like a family member in denial of his own teachings.

I had seen enough. My body was shaking, and I wanted out of the Vatican as soon as possible. I reached the door and took a big breath of fresh air and began to recover.

CHAPTER 8

# In the Footsteps of Saint Francis

The next day our small band of pilgrims left Rome by train for a monastery in the mountains of Northern Italy. When we arrived at the monastery, I was so glad to be out of the big city, and into the countryside. It was October and the trees were changing; a firework of color splashed the mountain terrain. From the monastery orchard I looked down to the valley below, a patchwork of grape vineyards dotted with village cottages. I wanted to walk and get some fresh air.

I took a path up the mountain that followed a small stream. The smell of rich, moist mosses filled my head. The sound of a small waterfall beckoned me up the path, and the smallest and sweetest wildflowers spoke to me as their heads bowed reverently to earthen floor that I gently treaded upon. I picked just a small bunch of wild cyclamen and a handful of wild thyme, and I sat down in a clearing. The sunshine came filtering through like rays of light come down from Heaven. As I sat quietly absorbing the sweetness of the tiny flowers in the palm of my hand, I breathed in the perfume of the aromatic wild herb. The spirit of Saint Francis touched me and I heard these words: *"More Precious than silver, more precious than gold, are the seeds of the Earth and the secrets they hold." This statement was my truth and the truth lay in the palm of my hand in these precious wildflowers.*

At the monastery, I was given a room to myself. It was simple cell, in traditional Franciscan style. It was quiet and had a view from the window to the courtyard garden below. People had gathered here from different countries to join together on a pilgrimage to Assisi. We would be traveling to various shrines where Saint Francis had journeyed and prayed in his lifetime, and much of this pilgrimage would be made in silence.

We gathered together for morning and evening prayers, and ate our meals together; the first morning the group came together to say the rosary. The pilgrimage leader needed a German translator, for the main part of the group was German, along with a few French people and three Americans.

In the center of the group, a beautiful altar was constructed, filled with roses and pictures of Mary and Christ. We each added our own personal sacred objects, such as rosaries, and little statues and pictures of Saint Clare and Saint Francis. Photos of loved ones also made up a part of this international altar. Then we picked up our rosaries, and rounds of Ave Maria began. It was an exquisite chorus of voices, each in its own language—German, French, Italian, English, and Swedish blended as one universal prayer to the Mother. It reminded me of my first dream of the rosary, hearing people saying it in all languages. The sweetest of the prayers was like a mantle of healing that engulfed everyone there. I floated out of the gathering as if I had angel wings.

The first stop on the pilgrimage was the shrine of Greccio. High above an Italian village, a monastery was nestled on a sheer cliff. Here the first nativity scene had been celebrated after the birth of Christ. We entered a small cave-like dwelling, and there stood a simple stone altar with a fresco of the Virgin Mother bare-breasted and feeding the Christ Child. Next to this was a painting of Saint Francis holding the Christ Child as he knelt at the manger.

In Greccio the Christmas-crib tradition began, initiated eight hundred years ago by Saint Francis. Christmas was approaching, and Francis, being the exuberant saint that he was, wanted to make this day special. But because he had taken the vow of poverty, he needed help obtaining the needed materials, so he asked a man (named John Veltia) to assemble the needed stable, manger, and animals for the celebration. He supplied all that the saint had asked for.

As Saint Francis celebrated the nativity, a vision of the Christ Child in the manger appeared: The people saw Francis holding a newborn babe. The fellow monks preserved the hay from the manger, and it was used to heal the mules and other animals. After this miracle, this tradition became widespread throughout Italy, France, and Germany. Master craftsmen would spend all year carving figures of the Holy Family, and the churches would display the figures and the Christmas Crib with Jesus. On St. John's Day during the summer solstice, master herbalists would gather herbs and plants—which became known as the holy hay or cradle grasses—and the very finest of these would be saved and then placed into the crib with the Christ Child.

\*\*\*

Next to the shrine, a modern church had been built, and, once inside, I was amazed at all the carvings that decorated the church walls. But what struck me most was a sculpture of the Virgin Mother over the altar: A white porcelain image of the Mother with a golden halo surrounded by golden lilies was imbedded into a blue rim that looked like an open vagina. This was the piece above the main altar! This holy shrine embodied the sacredness of birth—and the healing of the inner child, as I discovered there.

The night before coming to this holy shrine, deep and painful inner-child issues had emerged from my subconscious. *Now, as I knelt before the Christ Child altar, they were washed away in a moment of grace.* I realized that the Christ Child image was a powerful archetype useful in healing the inner child.

\*\*\*

The next mountain shrine we visited was where Saint Francis had gone to recover when he was very sick. We came to cave dwellings at the top of a winding path up the mountain. A small shrine of Mary, which had been hung from a tree branch, brought even more beauty to this setting in nature. A small chapel built of stone sat at the top of the mountain, and Francis's sickbed had been placed in a small chamber next to the shrine. I went in and knelt by the altar, and that same old, visionary feeling came upon me, and I started to see.

*A knight was standing next to the altar. He was wearing chain mail, and underneath he wore a black and red tunic. He had dark hair and a black beard; he wore a helmet and carried a sword. He was the inner protector of this little chapel.*

*I got up and peaked through the window where Francis's sickbed was, and I heard the spirit of Francis speak to me. "Even in my suffering I was with God. Teach those who suffer that God is with them."*

Silently, I made my way to the caves of Francis and his brother monks. Some of the caves had automatic lights that went on when a pilgrim entered, however, one cave did not. It was cold and dark, but I could see in the dim light where an altar once had been, long ago. *I put my hands on the cold rock and I heard, "For all those who come into the darkness of the soul, I will give you my illumination and understanding. I will shed my light." From the corner of my eye, I saw something that reflected a glimmer of light. I picked it up, and there in my hand was a small rock crystal.*

I left the cave and joined the others, who were outside roasting wild chestnuts on an open fire. I ate to my heart's content, and the day was done.

***

The next stop on our pilgrimage was a shrine where Saint Francis had a vision of an angel. This angel came to him while he was in deep prayer.

When he was younger, Francis had had a very wild and carefree life. He'd had many women—in fact, he was something of a medieval playboy. Then, he went away to war, was captured, and was put in prison. After being released, he became very ill, and when he recovered, he saw the world differently.

He had come from a wealthy merchant family of Assisi, and the first inklings of his awakening gave him compassion for those who suffered in poverty. His eyes became open also to the God Spirit that was clothed in the natural world. These were the events that pushed him into the search for God Union.

This holy place where we had gathered was where an angelic messenger gave Francis absolution; his sins were forgiven through divine intercession. The word "sin" in the Christian context is loaded with thought-forms of guilt and eternal damnation, but the original meaning came from archery. When a bowman aimed at the center bull's eye and missed, he was said to have sinned. Therefore, when one is off center, one has sinned.

The essence of divine forgiveness was the foundation of this holy sanctuary we were about to enter. At the bottom of the steep path to the shrine, the group leader informed me that this was a place to pray for oneself and all those in one's life.

This seemed especially appropriate for me, because one important thing I had recognized in myself and in others was the interconnectedness between us and our families, through the genetic patterns that are passed from one generation to the next. Some of these patterns can be gifts or talents but others can take the form of habitual negative thinking or actions. When the soul incarnates into its physical vehicle, it is clothed by the flesh of the mother, and within this flesh, blood, and bone all the ancestors of the past are living, and are carried on in the DNA.

Native Americans recognize this, as traditionally they pray for their ancestors—the seven generations before them and the seven generations behind. Modern psychiatrists have learned to help people see their childhood and genetic patterns, but often, patients know their patterns but remain stuck repeating the same old programs. I have found in my own journey that psychological understanding is required in order to break through conditioned patterns, but it is the grace of Spirit that removes old conditioning completely.

My own life has been an interesting experience genetically, for I am the proud mother of three children, each of whom has a different father. Many patterns that I have witnessed in the family structure I do not want repeated in my children's lives. Things that I have suffered I do not want passed on. At times, I have made it my practice to pray for the clearing and untangling of unwanted genetic patterns, and now, here, was the perfect shrine to pray for the family line. This was what I planned to do.

Armed with my quartz crystal and amethyst rosary, I was ready to make the trek up the mountain. I crossed myself and began my prayers, and I *felt* my grandmothers and grandfathers. I repeated my Ave Maria, and after each prayer, I offered one of the grandmothers or grandfathers on the altar of my heart. I asked that any transgressions that they had made in their lives be completely forgiven and dissolved. I could feel both of my great-grandmothers walking by my side.

When I had gone through my own family line, I focused on my eldest son's father's lineage. The prayers went deeper and I concentrated on problems that were part of my son's genetic patterns. I repeated this process with each of my children's lineage and offered up mother and father, grandmothers and grandfathers, back into the great-grandparents and the great great grandparents.

The path became steeper and the genetic load I was carrying up the mountain felt like a ton of bricks. I did not stop my prayers, but dove deeper into prayer for the family line. When I reached the top, I was both physically and spiritually exhausted.

I walked into a little stone shrine and silently sat down. I laid my prayers and family burdens down at this holy place. It was as though I had carried a bag of rocks up the hill and then let go of all the weight when I sat in the power and presence that this sanctuary offered. I could feel eight hundred years of prayers and tradition that had come before me, and it felt like a vortex of light that I could step into and be bathed by its radiance. I felt this had been created by the prayers of pilgrims who also had knelt in silence in front of this simple stone altar. It was a huge release.

Though this was not the first time I had prayed for the family line in such a way (in fact, there have been periods when I prayed for months in order to help diminish family genetic karma), when I walked back down the mountain, I felt uplifted and spiritually accelerated.

CHAPTER 9

# Visions at Assisi

We traveled north through Italy into Assisi. This picturesque village built around a hill above olive orchards and vineyards was where the magical lives of Saint Francis and Saint Clare—his female counterpart—took place. They had such a burning love for each other that in one incident, the monks at the monastery, thinking there was a forest fire, found instead that it was Francis and Clare engulfed in the fire of spiritual love that lit up the whole forest.

Clare was much younger than Francis, but after hearing him preach in the streets of Assisi, she left her aristocratic life and, like Francis, took the vows of poverty and chastity. Francis and Clare were the rebels of their day, bringing revolution to the Church and the families of Assisi. They both had come from the elite of their society, and their choice to live in poverty became a strong statement to the community; the cream of the crop of Assisi's youth left their homes, their families and their wealth to live with Francis and Clare. To understand this, one must know that at this time, the Church fathers were living in decadence and accumulating wealth while the poor were left in hunger. Wealthy landowners did not provide well for those in the working class. People were hungry, many suffering as serfs. Francis's and Clare's lives were a revolution in themselves, to create in the Church and its members an awareness of the mercy of generosity.

Like many in Eastern and Western spirituality, Francis and Clare took a traditional ascetic approach of depriving their bodies sexually, as well as living in poverty. In spite of this, I feel they both attained enlightenment, and their spiritual presence is available today in Assisi for those who have the inner wisdom and receptivity to receive what is spiritually recorded there. But, perhaps it is because of their denial of their bodies that they both, later in life, suffered many illnesses. Francis often had to be carried by brother monks to the mountain retreats because he was too weak to walk; Clare spent much of her life bedridden. Even though asceticism has been a path to God in the past, a new consciousness is trying to be born on this planet: the consciousness that recognizes sexuality as a part of God and the body as a temple of the Spirit.

Francis's and Clare's vows of poverty also were perfectly appropriate for their time in history, for they created a revolution of awareness within the Church. But now, something new regarding money is also trying to be born: a new vision and responsibility of using the power of money spiritually without greed, and with a balance between giving and receiving. Money, sex, and power all need to be spiritualized, and this is the challenge of living in the present day. God is everywhere and in everything; no separation is necessary as we merge into a new understanding and bring a spiritual presence to all aspects of our lives.

*** 

At the hotel in Assisi where I shared a room with the two American women I had been traveling with, we all gathered downstairs to eat lunch. We took each other's hands to say grace. *My spirit soared above the earthly scene, and I found myself above the town of Assisi where angels were circling, singing praises to God.* I knew right then how holy this place was. So many prayers daily are being said by monks, nuns, and pilgrims that the angels themselves are ever hovering over the village of Assisi.

After lunch, when we had some free time, I went out into the street. Here, where there were houses built in a pinkish-colored stone that had quarried nearby, the street under my feet was smooth cobblestone. I could feel in the very stones the prayers of all those who had come before me to this sacred place. This feeling made me completely grounded as I stood there saying my own prayers, adding them to the accumulation of all the prayers said prior.

There were so many places to visit in this small town, for at every corner there seemed to be a church that contained some bit of history of Francis or Clare. Every day, when five o'clock came around, I would go to vespers at the window of St. Clare, in the convent.

The convent door was open, and behind a maroon velvet curtain I entered a small room peopled with nuns who ranged from the very young to the ancient. Displayed at the altar was a monstrance with the Eucharist representing the Body of Christ. On the ceiling above this small chapel were frescoes of four angels and on the wall before me was a painting of Saint Clare at a window. I was told that many people have visions here of Saint Clare.

I knelt on a hard, wood kneeler with no padding, which immediately moved me into that ascetic domain, and began to pray to Christ. The nuns were singing in Italian, their voices making soft music, and sweetness filled the atmosphere.

*The Eucharist began to glow golden before my eyes and the Christ Presence took my body and soul into an orgasmic union with the Divine. I felt completely at home, I felt the power of the Body of Christ, and I felt that everyone was a part of that presence. I melted and all that seemed left of me was the desire to feel Christ's presence in the deepest recesses of my heart. I was flying with the convent girls!*

\*\*\*

Every morning on our tour, the teachings, and the gathering of the pilgrims, would begin, but it was in my free time I found my place in Assisi. I could walk anywhere and visit the shrines that personally spoke to me. Six o'clock in the morning would be a double cappuccino, and then I would trot down to the Church of San Clare for seven o'clock mass. The only other people in the street would be the stonemasons with their buckets of tools, going to work to restore churches and buildings that had been standing for hundreds of years.

Once inside the Church of San Clare, I liked to visit the tomb of the saint. Down in the crypt, Saint Clare was laid out, still preserved, under glass; her body never decomposed. This was the first time I had seen such a relic, and I wasn't so sure I wanted to see some corpse! *But when I viewed Clare's body behind the iron bars that were there to protect her, I immediately connected to her spirit and I heard a voice say to me, "Do not let the body be a prison, but let it be the temple of the Holy Spirit."*

I then made my way up the stairs of the crypt and went to morning Mass. When I walked in, from behind the wall of the altar I could hear the heavenly voices of cloistered convent sisters, singing. After the Mass (which was said in Italian), I went to pray in front of a very old painting of Saint Clare, and as I knelt in deep prayer, I heard a group of people come and join me, in silent prayer in the pews behind me. I didn't turn around, but stayed with my devotion. *I could feel the power of the prayers of those sitting in silence behind me. When I got up from the kneeler to leave the church, I saw that no one had been there except the Invisible Presence, the members of the Body of Christ.*

***

During my last days at Assisi, I visited the Basilica of Saint Francis, which is where Francis was buried. One of the reasons I chose to visit this shrine last was because it was against Francis's wishes that it was built; he asked that he be buried in the potter's field where the poor were laid to rest. Our pilgrimage group walked silently through the streets of Assisi on our way to the basilica. Many of the pilgrims had bonded with each other, and held hands in their newfound friendships. But, as for myself, I had entered such a deep place of silence within my soul that I kept very much to my self. Even after the pilgrimage was over, it was hard for me to come out of the depths within myself where I had traveled. I had gone so deep that I wanted to stay and never return to the everyday world.

The basilica was as long as a city block. Once inside, the beauty of the many frescoes that had been painted on the walls and ceilings fed our souls. We descended the stairs down to the crypt. White, long tapered candles were all aglow, representing the people who had visited and left their prayers in this sacred sanctuary. I lit a candle, whispered my prayer, and entered the tomb of Saint Francis. Many people sat in silence; others knelt in solemn prayer. I stood at the back wall of the crypt and began to go deeply inside myself. I stared at the huge cemented tomb of Francis and felt the heaviness of the basilica trying to enshrine the spirit of this holy man. All of a sudden a brilliant vision of Saint Clare blazed before me.

*She came in like a shining sun and within the brilliance I saw her face smiling and embodying the power of divine knowing. Then Francis appeared, like the Divine Fool he was noted as being. There he stood with his arms outstretched in the form of a cross, and perched on each were white doves. He began to dance and in his dancing the birds flew over his head. He began to sing, "I am not there, I am everywhere. Look for me in the trees, in the sky, in the blades of grass, in the center of every flower, in the center of your very own heart—this is where you will find me."*

My heart burst in his divine presence. My feet began to move with the spirit of his dance and I, literally, danced from his tomb up the stairs into the basilica above in joyous union with his saintly presence. I was in touch with the true spirit and freedom that this saint embodied. I was in his grace. I was bathed by his bliss. I waltzed through the church as if I owned the place, and for that moment I did.

Upstairs in the basilica was the main altar, but in both sides of the building were little alcoves that held shrines to various saints. I entered through the archway of one of these rooms, which had beckoned me, and there painted on the ceiling above me was Mary Magdalene kneeling, in her scarlet robe, with her long, streaming, red hair and her hands outstretched to the Christ. Her life story was depicted on the walls, her love of Jesus and her devotion to the Christ throughout his death and into his resurrection. It was beautiful in the simplest of one-dimensional paintings.

Directly across from Magdalene's shrine was the shrine to Immaculate Mary. This became my favorite place in Assisi. I came into the shrine and knelt in prayer. Old women dressed in black lace mantillas knelt beside me, and in their whispered Italian I could hear them saying, *Ave, Maria, piena di grazia il Signore 'e con te:* "Hail, Mary, so full of grace, the Lord is with thee." This was the only Italian I learned before the trip—I figured, if I knew "Hail, Mary" in Italian, I could go anywhere. I began to say the "Hail, Mary" with the other women as we all knelt before the statue. Mary's mantra was on my lips, repeated over and over until her presence filled every thought in my mind. All of a sudden, the statue began to glow golden.

*I rose up in my consciousness and was engulfed in her golden light. I was on the beam of light, and I felt I was riding on the light beam above my little, earthly body. I was bathed in her radiance. I stayed there for hours, not wanting to leave her presence. I was higher than a kite.*

Finally, I left and went to the hotel for a nap. When I woke up, I felt that the very cellular structure of my body had been changed and had been charged with light. I got up and went straight back to the shrine; I could not get enough of the presence that I had found in this holy of holies. I surrendered my life and myself to the feet of the Mother—I was hers and she was mine.

***

That my view of the Blessed Mother is very much different from that of the traditional Catholic Church does not change the *fact* of her existence. I have sought out historical truth in order to understand her divine presence more fully. And, the fact that historically the Church has been influenced by politics, and has manipulated the truth, does not lessen the power or the presence that the Blessed Mother brings. Every world-power structure—whether secular or religious—is tainted by the mind of the human condition. The purity one seeks is found only in the inner sanctuary of the soul: This needs to be remembered. For the way God/Goddess comes to man and woman is through the human vehicle. We are God's hands and feet. Remembering this, one has to take into consideration that the human element is always there, coloring the experience, and that this is the way we learn. The deepest experience of the Divine I have encountered is where all thought and form disappear, all dogmas and doctrines fall away, and the silence and void become pure energy: nameless, faceless; it just *is* and is *not*. It is God and is nothing, all at the same time. Even my own visions and my own experiences become like paper dolls that fall away in the presence of the Silence. Words cannot touch it, no proof is needed for its existence, for it just *is* and ever will be.

***

I could not contain the beauty of my vision at the shrine of Immaculate Mary, and I shared it with my roommate, Mary Kay. I brought her to the shrine, and we knelt in front of the golden presence that was funneled through this statue of Mary. I wanted so much for Mary Kay to see the beauty through her own eyes. "Mary," I prayed, "show Mary Kay this vision." Even though Mary Kay couldn't see the vision, she felt the immense energy that was being poured forth at this holy place. Then, after she snapped a few photographs of the statue, we left. The pilgrimage was coming to an end, and it was time to say good-bye to Assisi.

\*\*\*

I returned to my home and family in California. I should say, my *body* returned—it took months for my *mind* to come back from my experiences. Everything had changed. My old life as I had known it needed to be transformed. My entire world was different.

A week had gone by, and I was puttering with my plants out on the back patio, cleaning out my home shrine to Mary, with its statue of her. My eldest son had brought this statue back to me from Mexico when he was about twelve; he had carried it with him, wrapped in an Indian blanket. It was one of the nicest gifts I had ever been given. Made of terra cotta, she sits on a crescent moon with a crown that is removable. I remember sitting by her in the garden that day, making the sign of the cross, and praying, *"In name of the Father, in the name of the Son, and in the name of the Holy Spirit."* Immediately I heard, *"You forgot the Mother. How can there be four points of the cross and only three holy names mentioned?"* I repeated the sign of the cross, reaching my hand to my forehead and saying, "In the name of the Father"; bringing my hand to my belly, saying, "and the Mother"; and finally crossing my hand from one shoulder over to the next and adding, "and the Son and the Holy Spirit." It was time the Mother took her rightful place and was recognized as the divine, feminine aspect of God.

*All of a sudden, I felt the energy pour down upon me and I fell to my knees in front of my home shrine. I was speechless. I couldn't move, because it was so strong a wave of bliss that had come over me. It felt so much like my experience at the Immaculate Mary shrine in Assisi that it brought tears to my eyes.*

Finally, I regained my composure, and got up off my knees to go check my mailbox. There in the box was a letter from Mary Kay and, inside, a series of photographs. Three were of the Mary shrine at the basilica: The first was a picture of the statue, showing nothing unusual; the second was of me touching the tip of the crescent moon the statue stood on; *and last, but surely not least, was a photograph of Mary glowing completely golden—just the way I had seen her in my vision state.* Blessed Mary had answered my prayers: She let Mary Kay see her in all her golden glory.

CHAPTER 10

# Divine Love

*Italy not only brought me spiritual transformation but also propelled my life into a major transition. My fifteen-year marriage was coming to a close. I had tried to keep the last remnants of the relationship, but it was becoming too obvious that we had grown in different directions and had different dreams to follow. It was time to let it go.*

The ending of the marriage opened me up to a new lifestyle and possibilities that suited me. I moved into the downstairs apartment of my girlfriend Elizabeth, giving me a view of the beautiful San Francisco Bay. During the day, I worked as a gardener, specializing in organic care of roses. Even though this work sometimes was physically taxing, it did give me hours of solitude, which helped me reflect on my life and the changes I was going through.

Elizabeth had recently been initiated as a priestess of Mary Magdalene, whose lineage came directly from southern France where the Magdalene lived after the crucifixion. (I find it very interesting that the many sects of the Catholic Church have traced their lineage back to the apostle Peter, who denied Christ three times during the crucifixion—while the Magdalene, Mother Mary, and Mary of Bethany remained with Jesus at the foot of the Cross.) The lineage of Magdalene comes from Magdalene herself and down through a society of women that had to go underground for centuries to avoid persecution. In the Gnostic writings, Magdalene was referred to as the apostle of apostles.

My friend Elizabeth's initiation as a priestess of Mary Magdalene was a very important moment in her life. She had spent many hours of research work tracing the footsteps of the Magdalene, and this saint had become Elizabeth's passion, sparking her goal to bring forth a new understanding of the scriptures. Her initiation gave her the right to conduct Mass in the Gnostic tradition. Needing assistance in serving the Mass, she chose some of us who had been in the woman's group to help her.

One day when Liz and I were alone, she wanted to give me a blessing from the lineage that she now carried. We began to make an altar together, and on it we put images of both Magdalene and Mother Mary. We placed roses from my gardens and a small bottle of anointing oil from a church in Italy by the pictures. A flask of holy water was added to the other sacred objects, and the blessing was about to begin.

Elizabeth has a very soft energy, which comes through her when she prays. The Divine Feminine flows through her like a sweet spring and caresses you with the gentle power of prayer. Elizabeth opened the bottle of holy oil, anointed my forehead, and began to pray over me. She repeated this process, anointing the palms of my hands, my eyelids, the center of my chest, and the bottom of my feet. In return, I prayed in the same way over her, that her work would fully flower. The blessing of the Magdalene was now part of me.

My old life had fallen away, and a new bud sprouted from what had seemed barren. A new life was waiting to be born. It was time for resurrection.

***

Elizabeth brought the group of women to a church on the San Francisco peninsula where a Gnostic Mass was celebrated every Sunday. The procedures are much like those of the Catholic Mass, but the Gnostic Mass seems far more joyous and alive in its celebration of the Eucharist. Women are allowed to become priestesses and to perform spiritual duties for the church.

We arrived at a very small chapel that had been converted from an office building—it seemed a highly unlikely place for such a "mystery school" to be located. But here it was, and our little group walked in and settled down in one of the pews. The residing priestess walked up the aisle to begin her sermon. She was quite beautiful:

Her dark hair fell to her shoulders, framing her dark complexion and warm brown eyes. She wore a plain, natural-colored robe with a burnt-orange veil loosely draped over her head and cascading down her shoulders. She was from France, directly from the lineage of Mary Magdalene. Her presence was not only filled with beauty, but also contained power. As she stood before her congregation and spoke in her thick French accent, I felt she had just stepped out of the catacombs. The soul wisdom she held was from a very ancient time, and it demanded respect.

She informed us that everyone was welcome to partake in Holy Communion—that one's religion or culture was not an issue, that it was up to each person individually to make his or her own choice whether or not to partake. Then, to begin the ceremony, four men walked up the center aisle, each carrying a pole over which a Bedouin-style tent was constructed. They placed themselves over the main altar and hoisted the tent over the altar table, holding it in place with their poles. To the side of the altar sat a woman dressed in white and completely veiled. I was told she represented the Veiled Sophia, or Veiled Wisdom. The priestess began the Mass by calling on the natural elements of nature. She honored the animals, all those under the sea and those who flew in the air and who walked or crawled on the land; it reminded me so strongly of what we used to do in the sweat lodge with the Native Americans. She then honored the trees, plant life, and the angels of water, earth, fire, and air. By this time I had slipped into another one of my altered states, and I saw on the etheric level what she had summoned. *A deer came and knelt by the altar. Whales and dolphins were present. Birds flew over her head. Many different animals were represented and all gathered under the altar's mantle and settled down for the celebration of the Mass.*

The priestess then referred to the Christ as the Beloved, and to his sacred spouse as Sophia; the Mass was the celebration of and the union with this sacred marriage between the two. And, just before we were to take communion, I had another vision, this one from another time in history that I was familiar with. *The ancient Egyptians' savior god Osiris and his sacred spouse, the goddess Isis, came into my inner world. As in the myth, he was dismembered, and his various body parts hidden in the Earth. Isis had such love for her mate that she searched for him and reassembled him with the help of her sister.*

*I experienced this as a memory but also as an active vision. It was as though this Egyptian myth overlay the Christ and Magdalene story.*

*I saw in all of the souls of the congregation the missing pieces of the Savior God. It was through Holy Communion that Christ was found within each person. My vision grew larger, and I saw the Christ in everyone. Everyone together made up the Body of Christ. The separation between each individual melted into unity through the act of Holy Communion.*

It was time for communion, and I went up to the altar to receive the body of the Beloved. I felt the Sophia had taken me under her veil and revealed one of her great mysteries.

✳✳✳

I had been visiting a Catholic church in San Francisco on Tuesday nights for Mass and a healing session. The church was run by the Franciscan order, and my time in this parish brought me back to Assisi. This church was unusual because, recently, on the outside wall of the church, an image of Mother Mary had been appearing.

One evening I had gone to the church with a girlfriend, her daughter, and my own daughter Selene. We pulled up in front of the church where the image of the Mother had been appearing. People were gathered around on the sidewalk, saying the rosary. The four of us got out of the car and began to stare at this image that was appearing and changing before our eyes. It was a silhouette of the Mother. When I first saw her, she appeared like Lady Guadalupe, but then the silhouette changed into Mary, with her arms outstretched to the crowd of people that were gathered around her. The final image I witnessed was of the three Marys gathered around the foot of the Christ's Cross. I wasn't the only one witnessing the visions; it also appeared to the females of our little group and to others standing on the sidewalk. Then, as the service was about to begin, we went into the church.

The church itself was beautiful. Above the main altar, instead the traditional crucifix, was an incredible statue of the Assumption of Mary. She did wear her blue mantle, as in traditional representations of her, so we could see her long, brown hair flowing down her breast. She stood upon a golden crescent moon that was nestled in a cloud with twinkling stars. The church had all the glory of the old Catholic Church that I remembered as a child.

The altar to the left was dedicated to Saint Francis, and the altar to the right was the Sacred Heart of Jesus. The four of us settled down in a pew behind four nuns dressed all snow-white habits—they reminded me of white doves.

The four sisters in the pew before me brought me back to the time when I was a child; the old-time flavor of the church adorned with statues and candles reminded me of my childhood spirituality. And during this time, my mother helped teach three nuns to drive. These sisters were very sweet and possessed incredible "prayer power." When I was with them, I learned first-hand how to pray and what prayer could accomplish. This was a time of childhood innocence and complete faith in the power of prayer. My knowing these three nuns instilled in me an understanding of prayer.

But stronger than these memories or the beauty of this church was the power of the Holy Spirit that was available to anyone sensitive enough to feel its presence. *As the priest began Mass, I saw the entire church being flooded with golden light—the angelic kingdom was at hand. Around the statue of Mary I saw the little faces and fluttering wings of cherubim; they were stacked up, one angel upon another, all the way to the ceiling of the church.* The power of prayer that the priest and congregation had developed created an atmosphere of healing. I was fed spiritually just by being present.

When the Mass was complete, it was time for the laying on of hands. Everyone lined up in the aisles to take turns being touched and prayed over. I was praying deeply at this time for my own feminine healing. I walked up the aisle with my daughter, and as I looked at Selene, my prayers began to deepen. I wanted a better life for Selene, a life in which *her* Feminine could fully flower. I went up to the altar and knelt down. The Italian priest was praying over part of the group that had come up to the altar, and a Filipino woman was laying hands on the other side of the altar. I knelt and waited, and I silently promised that if I could be healed, I would share my healing with other women. I bowed my head and when I looked up, the Filipino woman was before me. She placed her hand on my heart and on my head and began to pray with such power and force of the Holy Spirit, it nearly took me off my feet. She prayed on my heart and her hand shimmied and shook over the center of my chest. "May your heart be open to more and more love, may Love Divine heal you in the name of Jesus," she prayed. Someone supported my back, for by this time I felt weak in the knees from the energy that was coming through and touching me, releasing my deepest core issues. When I got up and went to my seat, the tears of relief streamed down my cheeks. The dam had broken and love flowed through me as never before.

CHAPTER 11

# The Buddha in the Garden

Over the years, as I walked the path of my spiritual longing, I found that each religion or spiritual practice had its own roots in truth and its own respective powers. Different religions offered different aspects of the Divine. The Native American path helped me realize the Spirit behind nature. Christianity in its purest sense taught me the compassion and the forgiveness of Christ. I found it always effortless and fluid to find the truth and power in different spiritual paths, and to harmonize them. I knew that God was everywhere and in everything. Separation was not an aspect of God.

***

The garden became not only my place of work, but also my place of prayer and insight. I was in a client's garden when one of these "inner sightings" took place. This particular client had organized one of the largest Buddhist retreat centers in Marin County. His and his wife's home was filled with the vibration of their meditation practices. It was a good place for me to work.

One day when I was up on the hill cultivating some low-growing junipers, a Buddhist monk showed up—on the etheric plane. He looked at me as I dug around the juniper, adding fresh soil and pulling out the weeds. Then he gave me a discourse, and this is what he relayed. *"There are people on this earth who move the world through their prayers and walk silently without ever being perceived by the eyes of others. Their prayers and power actually change events and lives, but few recognize them in their service. They are invisible and in this state, they are able to accomplish their inner work."* He then *looked down upon me as I knelt there covered in dirt and said, "This is good work," and he disappeared.*

CHAPTER 12

# Samadhi at First Sight

My parents lived in Weed, California, a small town located at the base of Mt. Shasta. Shasta was a place of spiritual pilgrimage for me; I had lived there in the seventies, and it was there the beginning of my inner searching took place. The purity of the mountain environment was food for my soul and a retreat from the hustle and bustle of my city life in Marin County, in the San Francisco Bay Area. I hadn't been to Shasta in awhile; it was time for a visit.

After arriving at my parents' house, I was settling in when my mother knocked on my bedroom door. "I want you to meet someone who is doing a job for your father; come upstairs," she said. I went up to the kitchen, and at the table sat a man with reddish hair, with golden-blond highlights. He had those eyebrows that turn up on the ends, as if he'd just came out of a wind storm. My mother made a casual introduction, introducing him as Andreas; he spoke to me in English but with a German accent. I said hello, but at the time I was more interested in rummaging in my mother's kitchen cabinets; I was not paying much attention to what they were saying to each other. The next thing I knew, my Mother was informing me that Andreas had lived in India for five years—now she had my attention. Being the truth seeker I am, I wanted to hear what this man had to say and what had he gained by living in such a spiritual country. I walked over to the table and struck up a conversation.

What was said was not important, for only two paragraphs had been exchanged when I found myself spiritually being raised up into a state of *Samadhi* right there at the kitchen table. *All words ceased between the new stranger and myself, and I felt my eyes roll back into my head. The two of us hovered above my family's scene in the kitchen, with no words, no thoughts, just saturated in the divine presence of each other. I could feel this man's presence penetrate my soul as burning fire. He was hot and aflame with the Holy Spirit.*

By this time, my father had entered the room, and both of my parents stood looking at us in our spiritual state and began to wonder what had happened. I realized my family was still present, so I came down, back into my body, and tried to shake the feeling off and act somewhat normal.

Who is this? was my first thought. My second thought was, I've met powerful people before; so what? I went back to rummaging through the cupboards, trying to act casual about what had just taken place. But my body was on fire in his presence. I was caught off guard. It had been a long time since anyone had had such an effect on me, and it had never been quite like this in the first meeting. I tried to regain my composure. By this time my mother had stepped in, and began to tell Andreas about an event I was going to attend at a church in Mt. Shasta. She's ready to serve me to him on a silver platter, I thought. So, I said my good-byes and went back to my room.

It had been several years since I had interacted with anyone who had this degree of spiritual power. In fact, in my past I had been hurt by a couple of teachers who had reached a certain level of spiritual power, and I had made a decision not to "play" in the arena of spiritual teachers. This decision had had its effect on me in the past several years, and I was now pretty much on my own path, following my own inner prompting.

That evening I went over to Mt. Shasta, as planned, to a lecture—part of a series. When I entered the church, I saw Andreas sitting in one of the pews by himself. I was late—the lecture had started—so I slipped into the pew next to him. Andreas had his eyes closed, and I knew he was going into meditation. I closed my eyes and joined him. What took place in the next few moments was beyond anything I had ever experienced with another human being.

*Immense spiritual power just poured down over the two little bodies sitting in the pew. The power was so great that I began to climb in consciousness with Andreas's soul.*

Andreas took my hand into his, and that was when things really started to happen.

*A spiritual fountain rose from the base of my spine and traveled upward with such a force and power that it shot out the top of my head like an explosion. It didn't stop there but kept rising like a fountain of light and spilling over and showering both of us, and it just kept on climbing to even higher levels of consciousness. This fountain of spiritual energy took me into a state of ecstasy and I began to become orgasmic with each new level I passed through. It then reached to what I have experienced before as the source of my being, the God Head—the Goddess Head. From this ultimate, the energy then showered over us like a waterfall of grace.*

The power began to descend and it came down through our bodies and joined us together where we were holding hands. We both had gone so deeply inside this experience that we had lost track of what was going on in the program. Someone announced that a spiritual initiation was being offered; Andreas and I looked at each other and I said, "I think we already got ours." Andreas got up and walked out the door, and I was right behind him.

Once we were outside in the fresh air, I realized I was totally wobbly from the experience. My mind began to race, to try to grasp what had happened. "Who are you," I asked, "and what is your lineage?" I realized I needed to sit down; I wasn't stable on my feet. We walked over and sat under two incense cedar trees that were joined together at the base. The night was starry, the moon was full, and the power that had been switched on was not about to stop. I asked again, "What is your spiritual lineage?" Andreas replied in his German accent, "I am a bit of a stew." The words stopped there and I seemed to fall into a silence that no words or thoughts could erase. We looked into each other's eyes, and all that existed was the power of God between us, in us, and all around us. I turned around with my back to Andreas and closed my eyes, and I went deep inside myself.

He began to rub the tension from my shoulder blades that had developed from the intense downpour of energy. My body began to release from the touch of his fingers. But the release created space for even greater energy to pour in. He then worked on my head and the back of my skull. *I started to see colored pyramid shapes rise up and out from the center of my brain into the air above my head. My breath became irregular; an even greater release was taking place in my body. I leaned back into Andreas's chest, and it was as though his whole body had become my throne, and I felt incredible power showering from above us. Then, in all its brilliance, I saw a crown being placed on the top of my head. I was literally sitting upon a throne and being crowned. I felt myself at the seat of the very center of Andreas's heart. I felt I had been enshrined in his heart by the intense love between us.*

He had such power surging through him, his whole body stiffened like a male erection. My hands moved backwards and grabbed the top of his head, and the energy whipped through us like lightning bolts. I was in for a ride. I turned around and looked at him, my eyes closed, to feel the presence that was between us. There was only the silent void surging with power beyond this earth. Our meeting was like an atomic explosion of cosmic energy that I had only felt in my very most heightened states of consciousness, and never had another being catalyzed such a direct experience in me.

He looked at me and kissed my eyelids. Whoa, baby, I wasn't ready for this! I began to panic. What is happening with this man? I don't even know him! I wanted to run away, and that is what I did: I got up and said I had to go. Every part of my body was in shock. Andreas said, "Can I call you?" I replied, "I don't know what happened, but I do know that everything in my life is going to be different after this night." I got into my car and slowly drove off. And, even in my driving I had to be careful—I was totally altered and never the same again.

When I returned to my parents' home, I could barely speak, and I sure wasn't about to share what had happened—I didn't even understand it myself; it had taken me outside and beyond the scope of my inner experiences.

I went downstairs to shower; maybe by washing it off, I could find ground, I thought. My father, being very intuitive, came downstairs to ask if I was all right. "Yes," I called out from the bathroom, even though everything in my being was in shock. Then, as a "security blanket," I decided to sleep upstairs in my childhood bed. I crawled into my bed hoping I might sleep. But that was not about to happen.

The experience I'd had started happening again. *My inner being, from my lower chakras at the base of my spine up to the crown of my head, was lit up like a Christmas tree. It was like the lights at drag races that light up from the bottom and one by one turn on until a whole column of lights is turned on to start the race. I felt like my soul had just been plugged into a light socket and electricity was running through me. At the same time I could feel the presence of Andreas inside of me. I had total telepathic communication with him. I kept saying, "Let's just chalk this up as one of those guru experiences."*

I tossed and turned, and didn't sleep at all, and the next morning I found it impossible to eat.

The inner fire that was ignited, the Kundalini, was activated in my body like it had never been before. That morning I was calmer but did not fully realize what was happening to me. To help put things in perspective, I went to visit a girlfriend in the area. She had a sound studio and dance area in her home, and when a couple of other women arrived also, we began to dance and do "toning" together. Toning is making sounds that come from deep inside, and letting out whatever sound comes. This was the scene: four women dancing around wildly and making incredible music together. I always have loved to dance and have used dance to express my inner nature, but it seemed that over the past years I had lost this part of myself. Because of a heavy work schedule and responsibility, this part of myself had not had expression for a long time. It was refreshing to be moving again, and after the evening before, I had a lot to release and express.

At first I was interacting with the moment, with the other women, but then something happened: The Kundalini was activated to such a degree that it controlled my body and I had to just let this cosmic force have its way with me. The moment became ecstatic; then the power was surging through me at such a level that all I could do was lie down and let the energy "do me," and in allowing that, I became orgasmic. I felt Andreas inside of me, and I knew that this energy was connected to him and to what had been stimulated the night before. The power surged through different areas of my body, releasing in orgasm. The power would move to between my legs and I would climax. It would move to my heart and I would climax again.

It would shoot out from the top of my head like fireworks. I was out of control, but I loved every minute of it.

This state continued for a few hours until finally I had composure enough to drive home. When I got to my parents' house, I found out that Andreas had been there bearing gifts, and had just left. My mother handed me flowers and said, smiling, "You made quite an impression on this man." I thought to myself, "Is *that* an understatement!" I went to call Andreas to thank him for the flowers, but when I got on the phone, all my composure went right out the window. I heard his voice and I could barely respond to his conversation; I became like a young girl, embarrassed and tongue-tied. We decided to meet before I left to go back to Marin County; I would meet him the next day at his home.

The next morning, I found his apartment and nervously knocked on the door. Andreas answered the door, and this time we both were ready to talk. Andreas began the conversation by talking of his reflections on the past few days' events. "The natural synchronicity of our meeting, if it has any meaning, should be sought out on the level of our spiritual work," he explained. He continued, "The resulting chemistry would create such beauty and radiance as it would be hard to pray into existence by only one person."

I still didn't know what to think. I had not digested what had taken place inside of me. All that I was sure of was that it was the strongest connection I had ever had with another human soul, and I was affected.

Being this close together felt like two powerful magnets that couldn't be pulled apart, but outwardly, physically, we were still quite reserved. Just a glance across the room from Andreas, though, would put me into an orgasmic state. We sat cross-legged in front of each other and melted into each other 's presence. He placed his middle finger on my third eye and moved it quickly in a stimulating motion. I went through the roof! It was as if my third eye had become my clitoris. Andreas's stimulating of my third eye brought me to such a state of cosmic orgasm, I surrendered completely to his presence. Now, mind you, he had not kissed me, our clothes were fully on, and

I had not yet even fully embraced him in a juicy hug. But I was off and flying from the mere touch of his finger on my forehead.

Well, I then learned from Andreas that he had had much spiritual training in India. He surely wasn't like any of the other men I knew. He had spent much of the past twenty-five years meditating and practicing various yogic techniques. Many of the techniques were designed to merge one with the Buddha Presence—as far as I was concerned, he was flowering! He went on to explain what he felt had happened to us. "Prior to the point of meeting, both of us as individuals had reached our own degree of experience of what God Presence is. When we met, we triggered each other's God Presence into activation and thus the God Silence, or God's energy, descended in the most powerful way. We reinforced each other's God Experience, which became one God Experience exploding through two forms. A great degree of spiritual compatibility constituted the foundation whereupon this was possible."

Wow, I thought, this guy is deep. All I had been doing the past few days was roll around in bliss.

*We sat together in each other's silence, and his body began to stiffen. I was bathing in the bliss of being in his presence when he gently put his head down and touched the crown of his head to my heart-center. The fireworks were shooting off; it felt as though he had sexually climaxed from the top of his head into my heart.* If this was the Second Coming, I sure was glad I was there!

Then, we stood up and, casually, he showed me his apartment. He took me into his meditation room/bedroom. The room contained an altar and over it hung a huge picture of just the eyes of a beautiful, golden Buddha. I glanced at his bed, which looked luxurious, dressed in a soft, silky cover of cream and maroon. I was impressed, but I felt that, for now, it was a dangerous place for me to be with him. I wasn't quite ready to make that big, physical leap, even though every fiber of my being had already felt it. It was in wisdom to take things slowly.

It was time for me to leave. I needed to digest this experience, and five hours of driving down Interstate 5 was a good way to mull things over. Before I left, Andreas said, "I can't tell you what to do. You will need to see for yourself." I got in my car and drove away.

I wasn't even twenty miles down the road when I felt his presence burst in the center of my heart; in the very core of my being I found him. It was as if a sun had risen inside of myself, and that sun was Andreas's spirit. He had entered my heart in such a way that it was hard for me to differentiate between where God ended and Andreas began—it all felt like one being. This was the first time that I had experienced the Beloved within myself and outside myself simultaneously, with no separation. I must say that it was confusing, for in my previous experiences, outside myself was a lover, and inside myself was God and, more often than not, the actions of my lover on the outside compelled me to move *inside*, because of my suffering and disillusionment.

Now, for the first time, I was experiencing something totally different, and it took months for me to accept this new experience fully without being filled with the fear that I would get hurt. My past needed to die; everything that had gotten me to this point of God Experience was no longer valid—not in this new paradigm.

I drove down the road on automatic pilot, with Andreas's spirit inside my heart. I saw my whole life changing before my very eyes, and I knew that we had much to share and that this feeling and experience was not going to go away. He had entered through the inner temple door of my heart. It was from the inside out that I felt him and knew him like I had never known anyone before. I knew that he knew me, also. There was no need to convince him of who I was—he already had experienced me on levels that others had never flown to. He knew me better in two days than did others who had lived with me for years. I felt comforted, naked, and *seen*, all in the same moment.

When I arrived home, I went to the phone, called Andreas, and asked, "Are you my beloved?" "I love thee," were the words that I heard from the other end of the line. "You are my beloved in the most spiritual sense," he continued. He then went on to explain to me his experience after I had driven off. He said, "While it was perfectly clear to me from the very first moments that my life's flow was to merge with that of yours, the 'how' was not necessarily revealed immediately. However, when you left for the Bay Area several days after the first initial event of our meeting, my entire system went into shock. The recognition that our life was to be together went into full force."

Experiences in the next few weeks proved to me that this was not an everyday type of love affair. I could feel Andreas's presence with me during much of each day; this would manifest in the most peculiar ways. I would be driving to work in traffic when the spirit of Andreas would burst forth in my heart and I would have to find a place to pull over to have a heart orgasm. It was impossible to drive and to go through these experiences, too. So, I would be sitting there on the side of the road, with this massive amount of energy going through my entire body and peaking out and spilling over into ecstasy in my heart. My world and his had completely merged and, even though he lived three hundred miles away, there was no stopping the feeling and the power that we felt for each other. It was love, it was God, it was silence and, more than all the above, it was orgasmic.

The Kundalini in my system put me out of control. There were times when I was home alone that I would be rolling around on the floor, taken over by this power that pulsated through my spine. It burst forth in different centers of my body. It released energy in my system that had been penned up for years. It was as though lightning bolts were exploding in my genitals, in my heart, or in my third eye, and all taking place as I rolled around on the floor. I surrendered myself completely to the experience.

Talking on the phone, Andreas and I decided we needed to see each other again. He would drive down to Mill Valley for a visit, and I could hardly wait. I met him at the garden gate and brought him to my apartment. We gave each other a hug and I found myself melting into the silence. We had been with each other so much in spirit that it was almost unbelievable that we were here together in the flesh as we touched, body to body.

*We then sat together in meditation, cross-legged before each other. Andreas asked me to sit in his lap in a traditional Tantric yoga posture. (This is where the man sits cross-legged and the woman wraps her legs around his waist as she sits in his lap.) Well, I was in the hot seat—the closest, physically, I had let myself get to him. The fire went up my spine and out the top of my head into the God/dess Presence of spiritual union. My head tilted back naturally as the force and power surged through my body.*

*After meditating with each other, my body needed to lie down; it was physically taxing for this much force to flow through my physical vehicle. I lay down on the floor, and Andreas placed his hand on my womb and began to pray.*

"I call forth the power and the presence of the Holy Spirit and I give you my body. I call forth the power and the presence of the Holy Spirit and I give you my heart. I call forth the power and the presence of the Holy Spirit and I give you my soul. I call forth the power and the presence of the Holy Spirit and I give you my hands. And I ask for healing for the one at hand."

*I felt a surge of heat going into my womb that was soothing. There was no thought or even sexual feeling coming through at this moment—just a strong presence of God Power. I lay there and soaked up the prayers and the power that was being given.*

\*\*\*

*Andreas could not stay long, so he left to return to Mt. Shasta. Shortly after his visit, my daughter came home from school. We were standing together in the bathroom, combing our hair, when I felt my period coming on. It was earlier than usual, and I felt it must be that my system was cleansed from the healing I had just received from Andreas. I stood there with Selene in the bathroom, feeling blood trickle from my vagina, and in the same moment, Selene also started her period. It seemed that my healing had affected her cycle also, and that we were in sync together.*

\*\*\*

The three-hundred-mile distance between Andreas and me created time and space for this relationship to grow slowly. Our communication modes became phone calls, letters, and faxes—and we exchanged many. The spiritual connection that had been created in just a few visits was strong and present in spite of the distance. Innumerable times we would be on the phone, neither of us speaking. We were both bathing in the sweet silence of this union we felt with each other. I had never experienced this type of relationship with anyone to such a deep degree. It was as though we both became hollow reeds that the Divine rushed through. Attaching words or concepts to this incredible power is fruitless, for I was in an experience beyond this earthly realm. I was bathing in divine love with my consort.

CHAPTER 13

# The Anointing

During the days, I walked through my jobs and my life, but I was not alone. Andreas's presence was inside of me, and it could be felt. When I closed my eyes, I would fall into the bliss of communion with the Beloved.

We needed to see each other again, and it so happened Andreas had a business meeting in the East Bay. He would be staying at a friend's apartment for the weekend while she was away. We decided to spend the weekend together. I was excited, I was scared, and I didn't know what to expect.

I drove across the bay to Walnut Creek where he was staying. I knocked on the door and when he answered, I knew that this time there would be no holding back from the consecration of this union on the physical plane. We had merged together and felt what others only mimicked through sexual union. But it was now time to experience this union on every level; I was ready.

First, we walked out through the alcoves of the apartments where Japanese gardens were growing. We sat on a bench in front of a pond. I was nervous—I had not been with another man sexually since leaving my fifteen-year marriage. Andreas and I fit together in the spiritual realm, but would it be as good in the physical?

Andreas began to explain his unique sexuality, which seemed to explain the magnitude of some of the experiences I was having. When he lived in India in the mid-seventies, he was given Tantric teachings and practices, and, with the woman he was with during this time in India, he had experiences similar to those he and I were having. Both he and she were taught by a Tantric master and from these teachings and the practice, many spiritual experiences arose through their union. This had been twenty years ago and, even though he had other relationships and had been in love, this type of alchemy had not taken place again until he met me.

Tantra is the true weaving together of two souls in God Union. This type of Tantric connection is unusual and requires the right alchemy between two people for it to exist. My own experience prior to Andreas had been my search for the Beloved within myself; this did not incorporate a partner but was a lone journey. And, when I experienced this union with my Beloved within, it became an orgasmic experience with the Divine.

Andreas went on to further explain that in Tantra, you do not try to *make* anything happen; you do not have the goal of orgasm— neither for the woman nor for the man. He explained to me that he did not have a seminal emission during sex. On the physical plane, he went on to explain, it is necessary for the male to restrain himself from physical orgasm in order to nourish and to support the potential event of *spiritual* orgasm and ecstasy, which is beyond the body. In the man, the seminal essence is the most powerful storehouse of spiritual force. If the seminal essence is expelled, the gate of entry for powerful spiritual experience begins to shrink and disappear. Furthermore, Chinese scriptures state that the losing of *ching, or* "seminal life force," reduces his potential for extended longevity. In fact, certain Chinese scriptures go so far as to prescribe what constitutes a healthy number of emissions per week and per month for men of different age brackets, with the number of emissions reducing as the man grows older. With couples engaged in intense spiritual practices, for the man to have no emission at all is considered a viable possibility.

While there exist sexual mystery schools that propose that the woman restrain herself from the orgasmic experience for the sake of conserving and transforming her human sexuality into divine experience, it has been my observation that the restraint rules that apply to males simply are not applicable to females. Rather, deep orgasmic experience on the physical plane seems to act as a springboard into a most powerful, oceanic, divine experience for the female.

As we sat by the pond, I shared with Andreas some of my experiences with the healing of my womb and my sexual issues. I had touched on sacred sexuality at certain points in my life, but they were fleeting moments, and they never equaled in degree my experience within myself. The human element, and dysfunction, seemed to wear away the original spark that I had encountered in my relationships with men. Andreas replied by explaining that when a man ejaculates habitually with a woman, over time it breaks the energetic, electric, connecting charge between the two—that the ejaculation actually drains the man. Even if he truly loves a woman, he will feel he has had enough of her and needs space. This pattern is often seen in dating when a man is very hot for a woman; he chases her and as soon as she gives in sexually, he tires of her and runs off to the next female to conquer. The woman usually is left standing there, wondering what happened and feeling the man has run off with her energy. Of course, this is not love and is the extreme case, but the emitting of the semen breaks the connection between them. This explained some of the sexual encounters I'd had when I was single.

In Tantra, however, the circuit is not broken. My experiences with Andreas up to this point were of a Tantric nature. Even though we had not physically had sex, I had experienced sexuality to such a high level that a mere glance would set me reeling.

We went back to the apartment, and I made a small altar of the kitchen table while Andreas unfolded the couch that made up into a bed. I was nervous and, at the same time, very excited. We took off our clothes and lay on the bed. The phone rang and he answered it; it was for me. I crawled up over his naked body to get to the phone, and Andreas said, "Is this the way you are going to climb to God?" I smiled and took the phone call.

After the call, we settled on the bed cross-legged, looking into each other's eyes. The passion was burning but it was contained in the sitting and the silence. Andreas then took me in his arms and started to gently kiss me, first my fingers, then my eye lids, and sweetly on my lips. There was no hurry, he wanted to adore me and take me slowly. His slightest touch was charged with electricity. He used gentle strokes down my body, barely touching the skin. All the while, the passion was roaring under the surface of his slow, tender moments. Every part of my body he took time to kiss, my inner arms, my thighs down to my toes—nothing was overlooked or left out. My entire body became his loving terrain, melting at his touch and at the tenderness of his lips. At one point, when he was kissing my breasts, he fell into a state of such bliss that his eyes rolled back into a meditation state that lasted for many minutes.

*We both were intoxicated with passion, melting together, losing our egos and abandoning ourselves in the simple act of loving.*

I lay there ready and more than willing, when he sat up before me; my body lay sprawled over the bed, loose limbs, and all barriers melted and eager to take the plunge. I could tell he had slipped into a deep and altered state. He was in prayer, and I turned my attention inward and silently prayed upon our union. He then put his finger into the sweet female juices of my yoni and began to pray aloud. *"I call forth the power and the presence of Yesus Christos, and I give you our bodies, hearts, and souls. Bring a blessing to this union. Make it sacred."*

He took his fingers from the well of my Feminine and began to anoint himself with my juices. He brought his moistened finger to his third eye and to his heart and prayed upon our union. He then returned to the well of nectar and started to anoint me with my own life-giving juices. He touched my heart with his wet fingers, prayed over my body. Each time, he returned to my yoni, moistening his fingers and praying over me with my own female nectar. There was no thought or plan for what we were engaging in; it all was simply happening. I felt like a sacred honey pot being used to anoint us both for the most sacred. I lay there feeling the sacredness of my own female juices. I saw myself as a sacred wellspring; my very life force nectar became the anointing ointment for consecration to the Divine. I was in prayer, I was in union, and I realized the physical, sexual act that was about to begin was the most sacred act two souls could ever share.

\*\*\*

Andreas prepared for safe sex and then he took me into his arms, kissing my breasts, my stomach. He slowly worked down to my yoni and then silently and most reverently bowed his head at the opening of my pleasure gate. Never had I been treated with such love, tenderness, but most of all, sacredness. An image appeared in my mind; *I became an altar, my body the temple. This was not something that I was being told but was a vibrant, direct experience.*

He laid himself across my body and entered through my temple door with all of his manhood. There was no more Andreas, there was no more Raylene. We both had dissolved into the power that was pumping through the rhythmic motion of our bodies. Holding my beloved was like holding God. There was so much divine presence between us that all I could do was open wider and wider as he came into me deeper and deeper. His lingam became like a shaft of light that was in my womb but was also extended through my entire body into my heart. The feeling did not stop there but kept going into my neck and throat-center. Crystallized deposits in my neck began to break up. The shaft of light was being used like a laser beam, breaking through barriers in my throat and neck-center. He opened my mouth with his fingers as I began to climax, and whispered in my ear, "breeeathe."

It was all over—the years of suppressing my voice were released through my orgasm. Realizations began to bubble up into my conscious mind and I started to cry. The suppressed emotions from continuously being told "I do not want to listen" were unshackled and the crystallization broken through. The bones of my neck were cracking. Andreas held me and listened to what I needed to express, in between sobs. He was totally there in the moment and totally present for the event.

✳✳✳

I regained my composure. I felt more naked in front of this man than I had ever felt before. You could say that I was wearing my heart and emotions on my sleeve, but there was no sleeve to wear them on! I felt silence with him and I knew that anything that came up in me would fall away like a leaf in the autumn breeze, released, blown away, and accepted as naturally as our lovemaking.

He entered me again, but this time he did not hold back his passion. Now he took me wildly and freely and with the full force of the power that was between us. He drank of me like there was no tomorrow and flipped my body into positions and angles that heightened the sense of pleasure that I could receive. The energy that was funneling through us was like lightning bolts from the sky. I felt an electrical charge like we were on fire, and I felt I was in for one big meltdown. Orgasm after orgasm took place in me; there was no counting them, just the heightened peaks of ecstatic bliss. I was being driven to peak after peak until I totally surrendered one limitation after another. All the while, Andreas remained in a state of complete control, watching my every move, staring at me with the intensity of his eyes.

*My body melted into another image of the Earth. My breasts became the mountains, my curves the valleys. I could see trees growing all over me and bodies of water covered my body's terrain. He became a plow as he moved in and out, out and in; I felt I was a field being plowed. Beads of sweat rolled from his brow and they became the rain that watered my body's field. He was my sacred plow and I was the fertile field being made ready for planting.*

Not a drop of his seed did he release over the hours of pleasuring me. The orgasm would build in my womb like a hot, bubbling caldron and then would explode upward into my heart center and out the top of my head. Our bodies would go into a rest position and then I would feel the orgasm move into my heart and spill over like a goblet of flowing wine. It went on for hours; one experience after another with small rests in between.

\*\*\*

Finally, we decided to eat, for it was late afternoon and neither of us had eaten all day. When we found ourselves out in the world, we both realized that our consciousness had changed so dramatically that everything seemed surreal. Finding a parking place—even just driving—became out of the question for me. Andreas seemed much more grounded, so I let him drive.

\*\*\*

*Returning from dinner, we resumed in the apartment. This time the sexual heal-ing moved in a different mode. I was resting on the bed when Andreas put his hand on my stomach and started to chant "Sanjay Menla." (Sanjay Menla is the Tibetan name for the Medicine Buddha.) His voice changed octaves as he repeated the name Sanjay Menla. He moved his right hand to the opening of my yoni and his left hand to my heart. His voice deepened and the energy was pouring through my body like a steady stream of light.* My vision began to open up, and behind his left shoulder I saw a Tibetan monk chanting with him and ringing a Tibetan bell.

*I realized that even though I had reached a certain point in my own inner, womb work, my sexual being needed healing. I felt weakness in the lower part of my body compared to the strength that Andreas held, sexually and spiritually together. Even though I knew how to climb the heights on the spiritual planes, I had not totally integrated my spirituality into the lower portions of my body. His chanting went on for well over an hour; the sound of his voice was soothing and rhythmic. When he stopped, all that was left was silence. I got up from the bed and immediately started to feel very sick to my stomach. I went down to the floor feeling like I was going to let go of it all. Even though I was very uncomfortable in the moment, I knew it was part of the process of the healing. I had experienced this type of reaction before, in the sweat lodge.*

\*\*\*

One of the techniques that my sweat lodge teacher used after laying hands on people was to throw off the burdens of others by retching in the corner of the lodge; even though he never physically vomited, he went through this process to become free of others' bur-dens that he had taken on. This also, simultaneously, had happened to me several times during sweat lodge healings.

\*\*\*

Now, in the apartment with Andreas, I lay on the floor unable to move and feeling very nauseous, but I knew I was throwing off years of sexual blocks that I had carried in my body. The retching process stopped, my body was at peace, and when I breathed I felt like an open channel. I breathed and my breath seemed to travel from my nostrils all the way down to my yoni. Everything was open and the power of the breath flowed freely through my entire being.

We lay there and drifted off into a light sleep, entwined in each other's arms. When I awoke in the morning, I realized how weak my physical being was compared to Andreas's. I wondered if I could even keep up with him in such a sexual pace. It wasn't just the sexuality but the immense power that ran between us during the act. I shared my fears with him openly, and he looked at me and said, "Do you really want to believe that? Do you even want to go there in your mind?" "No," I replied, but I must admit I had my doubts. I felt I was strong, but that it took a new type of strength to contain such immense energies that flowed through us. "It's all new for you," Andreas replied. "It will take time to incorporate."

***

That morning I left to return to the Mill Valley house where Elizabeth was performing a Gnostic Mass. I walked in glowing with radiance. Elizabeth was standing there with my girlfriends Christy and Sabina; all were dressed in white gowns and each had a different colored veil over her hair. One look at me and they all knew what had happened. I was completely transformed by love and it was obvious to all.

Elizabeth performed the Mass, which is the reenactment of the Sacred Marriage, the Sophia finding the Beloved. When it was time for me to receive communion I stood in front of Elizabeth and Christy, completely open from all that had taken place the day before. The presence of God/dess flowed through my body. I knelt in front of her as I opened myself to receive the Body of the Christos. My body felt like an open chalice which was receptive to the communion, empty and hollow so the Divine could pass through me like the wind—overflowing in love, and feeling that I had been nurtured and fed spiritually and sexually like never before. All my Catholic-girl guilt and shame had fallen away, and I realized that the division between sex and spirituality that had been created for hundreds of years by the priesthood was created to hide the true power that could remove obstacles of all kinds. It was the power of creation. It was woman power and, when combined with the right partner, immense love, and the right attitude and spiritual understanding, it could heal, awaken, and uplift two souls at an accelerated rate.

Days went by before I saw Andreas again, but every night he would phone. The Tantric connection that we had developed was present even over the phone. We would talk awhile and then we both would fall into inner silence with each other. I could feel his presence within my heart. There were no words, no thoughts, just energy rippling through my body as I lay there with the phone at my ear. The feeling would build within me and my breath would become rapid, and finally it would spill over into an orgasm that centered in my heart. Andreas would go through his own experiences. During and after our phone conversations—or, better put, our non-conversations—he would fall into a deep inner state where every thought was cast into the void. He would disappear into a meditative experience, sometimes for hours. This gave a new meaning to phone sex!

Our experience of each other's presence had such a powerful effect on us that it catapulted each of us into inner experiences of the Divine. Neither of us was consciously directing the energy or trying to make anything happen to the other. Andreas would joke with me, saying, "I am not doing anything," but in the not doing, so much was happening for us both. I had no road map, no directions for this type of communion with another soul. But it appeared that the road map was written within our very bodies and souls, and that each other's presence unlocked ancient scrolls of the Sacred when we came together.

CHAPTER 14

# The Bedside Discourse

About ten days passed and we had to see each other again. We planned to take a trip up the California coastline together. Andreas drove halfway down from Shasta that evening and stayed in a motel before coming into the Bay Area. I woke up early the next morning; my body was sore from the week of garden work, so I jumped into the hot tub outside to soothe my tense muscles. I was floating around in the tub, looking up at the trees; a gentle rain was falling on my naked body, when I turned around and there was Andreas looking at me bathing in the tub. He smiled and said, "Perfect timing." I got out of the tub, my body steamy from the heat of the tub and the early morning air. Andreas wrapped a thick, terry cloth towel around me and we walked inside. I dressed, got my bags for our weekend journey and off we went up the Coast Highway.

We traveled until we came to a motel in the redwoods. An Indian family from Bombay ran the motel; Andreas talked a little to them about India, got the keys, and brought me to the room.

After settling in, we sat cross-legged in front of each other on the bed. Andreas started to run invocations on the motel room.

"I call forth the power and the presence of the Holy Spirit, I call forth the power and the presence of Jesus Christos: I give you this room, make it sacred. I call forth the power and the presence of Jesus Christos: Remove from this room all thoughts, emotions, and vibrations that are out of harmony with the Divine. I call forth the power and the presence of Jesus Christos: make this room sacred."

He snapped his fingers, and the very atmosphere had changed through the power of his words. "Now we are ready," he said, and he put his hands on my shoulders and began to invoke again.

*I call forth the power and the presence of the Tantric Buddhas, I give our bodies, our hearts, our minds, and our souls. I call forth the power and the presence of the Tantric Buddhas and I give you my beloved's body, heart, and soul to be initiated in the sacred arts of Tantric wisdom.*

As he said his words, I could feel power pour down and shower me from unseen realms. The downpour was immense. Tears began to stream down my face, for this new opening affected me to the very core of my being. So many of my experiences I will never be able to convey through words, for these types of experiences are removed from the realm of thought, and enter and touch you in places so deep that words are useless carriers of the message.

Andreas shared with me his dedication to invocation. He had realized at a very young age the power of calling the God Presence, or its various aspects. He had read Tibetan Buddhist texts and had come to the realization that statements such as "I pay homage to the Buddhas of the past, present, and the future" were not just literary niceties but in fact represented formulas that would vividly bring to life the tangible presence of the Buddhas that were invoked. Also, during his time in India, he was told that no Buddha ever dies. That it is through longing and a prayerful heart that any Buddhas can be accessed.

Andreas believes that there is a huge difference between positive affirmations and divine invocations. The former merely create a "groove" for personal manifestation of a thought, whereas the latter call forth divine power and, so, are aligned with prayer. If you look at the different religious pantheons, you begin to realize that there are different aspects of the Divine. Tibetan Buddhism has its eight Medicine Buddhas for healing. It also has Dharmapalas, which are wrathful deities that protect the Dharma. You can invoke the Laughing Buddha to lighten up situations in life. Then there is Green Tara, a female Tibetan goddess who has twenty-one different manifestations; she is a protector of people who are crossing the Ocean of Existence.

If you look at the Hindu pantheon, you see Shiva, destroyer of illusions and master of meditation. He can be invoked to help your meditation practices or to help you see through the veils of illusion that exist in the world of appearances. Or you can invoke Goddess Lakshmi to shower your financial world with abundance.

Then there is the pantheon of saints and angels in Catholicism. Saint Anthony is prayed to for lost articles. Saint Anne has the power of fertility. Archangel Michael flies in to protect, and to vanquish all evil. Saint Raphael, angel of travel, will keep you safe upon your journey. When you begin to realize that there are many different aspects of the Divine that can be utilized through prayer and invocation, you can see the similarity in the different religions—everyone is doing the same thing; it just comes in different flavors. What is important is that in invocations, you only use divinely realized beings such as Buddhas, masters, saints, or angels. It is through their divine presence that any problem or situation can be addressed.

Andreas has worked with invocations over the past twenty-five years, and one thing I noticed about him was how powerfully and importantly his words were used. He has the ability to cut like a laser through any given situation just through the power of his words. I also noticed he rarely misused his speech with coarse language or cursing. All of this pinpointed the fact that he had not only gained understanding about the power of the spoken word but he *embodied* the power of the word.

✻✻✻

"It seems that some of our best discourses are in bed, I've noticed," I said to Andreas. "I guess it's my bedside manner," he replied. It was getting dark and we took our clothes off and crawled under the sheet together and just held and melted into one another. He slowly and gently started to caress my body with light stokes up and down my torso. There was no rush, no pressure; he took me in slowly like an elegant eight-course meal, enjoying each phase of the lovemaking, taking pleasure in every part of me. There wasn't a part that was not caressed or given a small kiss or nibble. Lovemaking became an art form as we joined together in pleasure. He entered me and began to pray, once again invoking the Tantric Buddhas to bring their blessings to the sacred act we were about to engage in.

The merging and connectedness that I felt with this man were far beyond the physical sensations that I was experiencing. Prayers were interwoven between the shuttles of the sexual act. I realized how important are the thoughts during sex, for we literally lay upon the body of our beloved what we feel or think. When sex is engaged in with coarseness, resentment, and even anger, the partner absorbs these emotions. This can be done consciously or unconsciously. I think this is why many partners lose the feeling of sexuality with each other, because their sexual life is not a feeding but becomes an unconscious dumping ground.

In my own life, the thoughts held during past relationships had been absorbed by my body. The removal of these thoughts were addressed through prayer, so my body could become a receptive vessel for sacred sexuality. As Andreas shuttled in and out and out and in, the words "I love you" were repeated over and over. They became a prayer. I realized that his love was healing all the parts of me that had never been loved and never completely accepted. Not only did the orgasmic explosions happen repeatedly in my sexual center, but also the walls within my *heart* were crumbling and exploding into the void of my soul. The prayers were whispered aloud, the prayers were said in the silence of our own minds, but our bodies reacted fully to the beauty, power, and love that were generated as we made love.

CHAPTER 15

# Remembering Past Times

We fell asleep in each other's arms only to wake up again for new lessons in my Tantric Initiation. Again we began to make love. I experienced deeper surrender in the Divine Union with my Beloved. It was not surrender of myself to the personality of Andreas, but it was surrender to the Divine Essence of who this soul truly is. I couldn't tell what was spread wider—my legs or my heart as the opening that I was experiencing had gone past all barriers and blocks. I became a vessel of the divine in the very act of sexuality.

As we made love the power came through our breath and Andreas would breathe into my open mouth and I would be filled with his pranic essence. This breath took me to even subtler levels of the union that arose between us. His very breath of Life was moving me across time where I experienced no time. I saw my soul stretched out like a golden ribbon reaching over a sea of timelessness, where I had been with Andreas before in another lifetime. My soul cried out in agony " where have you been?"

*I literally felt my soul longing for the one before me. All of a sudden I saw myself being brought to him on a canopy litter that was decorated with flowers and sheer white curtains. I was younger with dark hair falling down upon a linen gown caught at the waist by a golden girdle. Four people carried the canopy to Andreas. He stood before me as a King in chain mail and a deep wine colored tunic underneath. I was being presented to him as his bride. In the next scene I saw us in the center of a large circle of standing stones. It was a moonlit night with a starry sky above. Sentries were posted in front of each standing stone as protectors, as we stood in the center of the circle. Their backs were turned to us as they guarded the area. Andreas slowly took my clothes off and began to make love to me in the center of this circle. I knew the lovemaking was for the benefit of the land and the kingdom. In the following scene we were in a castle and I saw druid wise men that had said blessings over us and put certain magical powers in us as a couple. The scene faded into a castle bedroom chamber with a warm fire in a stone fireplace. A large dog lay next to the fire. We were in a royal four-poster bed with crimson curtains and many coverlets for warmth. I felt such love for this soul that words cannot express.*

*In the next scene I saw that Andreas had gone out with an army of men and I was saying good-bye. When he returned it was on a stretcher. When I looked at him I knew he was dead. At this point of the vision I total lost myself in grief. I started to cry and sob. My very being was shaken by the experience. I felt this grief to such a deep degree. The separation from him during this lifetime had left me with a longing that lasted until I found him again. My body was shaken and I could not stop crying.* I opened my eyes from the experience and Andreas was alive before me. I clung to him still crying from the experience. Then he prayed over me, soothing me with the softness of his voice. I drifted into a deep sleep.

The next morning we decided to go to the ocean. So after breakfast we drove back towards Jenner. I sat in the car just feeling my body. Everything felt nourished in a way that I had never experienced before. It wasn't just that glow from the morning after but it felt like such a deep feeding for me.

We arrived at the ocean and walked down a narrow pathway to the beach. We strolled along the beach until we arrived at a secluded place amongst the rocks. I love the ocean. For me the sound of the crashing of the waves and the feeling of the sea air is totally exhilarating. I was playing in the waves as Andreas sat and watched me on the beach. I stood there communing with the spirit of the ocean, as I ran back and forth on the shore playing wave tag. I ran back onto the beach where Andreas was sitting and cuddled up next to him.

Andreas began to sing and the song turned from singing to chanting. My eyes closed and I rose up in consciousness from the sound of his voice. I felt our spirits rise together, soaring higher and higher, penetrating new levels of awareness like an arrow shot straight up in the air toward the sun. The sound of his voice was the carrier for our souls rising even higher. I felt my consciousness was reaching a pinnacle of awareness that I had never reached prior to that moment. We were there together as one. Then the power that we both felt began to descend back into our bodies. It flowed through my body and entered deep into the earth. It was ecstatic. It was orgasmic. Everything in nature responded in unison. It was not a disconnection from the peak of consciousness I was experiencing, but it was like bringing that peak awareness right down into the earth plane through my body. He sang. I experienced one inner orgasm after another. This experience of power was such a reminder of my first cosmic orgasm at the ocean over twenty years ago. The difference, however, was that I was experiencing it with another human soul. My divine lover now was given form. I never thought that this was possible.

Years of disappointments and disillusionments with love had been the motivating power that created my search for spiritual union with the Inner Beloved. Through my experience with various relationships I became jaded and disenchanted. I reached the point where I was ready to check into a convent. The idea became very appealing. But I continued to remember the vision of the sacred couples I had seen years before. That vision was now my reality and I realized that the healing between the sexes was completely possible.

By this time my body was adapting to the immense power that I was experiencing with Andreas. I did not feel the sensation of being wobbly or out of balance as I had before but now I felt I had integrated these new energies. We got up from our sitting place and walked to the car, passing people and enjoying the beach. I felt we held a sacred secret together as we walked among people.

I thought to myself if they only knew what had just taken place between nature and us. The ocean—she knew. The waves sang in unison with the slapping sounds upon the shore. The sea breeze—she knew, for she carried the song with her. The seagulls soared like our spirits. They understood such freedom. But the people we passed had no idea what had taken place. It was our secret. It was in our souls. I wish that everyone could experience such divine union, such divine love. The world would be an entirely different place. We got in the car and drove back to my house in Mill Valley. Andreas took the wheel.

He was in such a powerful centered space in himself that it reflected even in his driving. God was in charge and these were the vehicles that the spirit was allowed to work through. The secret was in the surrendering.

We arrived back at the house. We laid on my bed together before Andreas had to return to Mt. Shasta. It was hard to leave each other. It was like tearing two magnets apart. I lay in his arms and Andreas saw his own vision at this time and shared it with me. He saw me in a nun's clothing and he tore away my habit saying you now can have your inner beloved and me at the same time. The understanding of this vision revealed itself in the weeks to come as old patterns and habits were shed. False concepts, old guilt and shame fell away from my consciousness as my union with Andreas developed. My sexuality became sacred and integrated into my spiritual experiences.

Andreas returned to Mt. Shasta. I returned to my gardening and contemplation of all the changes I was experiencing. I missed him and it often was hard not to be with him all the time. But when I got quiet I could feel his presence in the center of my heart shining through like a brilliant sun.

The night after my oceanic experience I wanted to write my feelings down about what I felt about Andreas. I became very quiet and the spirit of Love Divine started to write through me, sharing with me wisdom about my current situation. I wrote within the pages of my journal these words:

"Let yourself love more than you have ever loved before. Let love take you where it is willing to take you. You are like a rushing river going toward the ocean of God Union. Do not build dams that will hinder this experience of love. Let not those who live on the river's edge influence this love. For they are not in the river. For they do not know its flow, its power, or the force to sweep away all differences for love's sake. Love and the river both have its purpose to move toward the Ocean of God's Bliss. Be not afraid of the power, do not be afraid of the force of the river. Let go and let love be.

Love, love, love—be the ocean of love that God meant you to be. Let all fears be washed away. Stand naked before me in the splendor, in surrender to God's love behind all forms and beyond all puritanical concepts. Be the flower God meant you to be, open and full of essence as you rise or descend. Know there is do difference, there is no sin."

I put my pen down. I closed my journal and pulled the coverlets of my bed over my body and fell into a deep and contented sleep. I was bathed in the essence of love.

CHAPTER 16

# The Wild Woman Set Free

The next meeting with Andreas was back at my parent's home. My mom and dad left for a few days at the coast and asked if I would house sit while they were away. This was another opportunity to see Andreas. I traveled up to Mt. Shasta, got settled in at the house of my parents, and said my good byes to mom and dad. I called Andreas on the phone and asked when he was coming over and would he like to have dinner. He let me know he had to finish his work but would be over afterwards.

The house my parents lived in was roomy and comfortable. My father had built this home with his own hands from the foundation on up. My mother had designed every little nook and cranny. The wooden A-frame blended into the natural setting of pine and cedar trees. The bedroom I liked the best was on the top floor. It had natural wood walls, a great view from the sliding glass door and a big brass bed covered with one of my mother's prized handmade quilts.

I went downstairs, poured myself a nice hot bath and slipped into the tub. When I would come up from the city to Mt. Shasta I loved indulging in my little water rituals. During the summer time I liked to stop at Soda Creek on the way into Mt. Shasta. This was where as a child I learned to swim in ice-cold glacier water. At other times I would enjoy a mineral bath at Stewart Springs. If I couldn't do one or the other it would be a long hot bath at my parents' house. Their well water was pumped up from underground caverns in the earth. I always personally felt that the best way to connect to the spirit of the mountain was to bathe in the water. As I sat in the tub, running the hot water, I would think of the underground rivers this water came from and the mountain's snow that had melted. I would reflect on the element of water and it's journey before coming to my bath. This was something I had done for years, the many times I had returned to my mountain home. I thanked the water for its gift and I just let my body soak. I relaxed and let the water cleanse me of city life. Now I was ready for the mountains and the visit with Andreas.

Evening was approaching and Andreas knocked at the door. I was more than ecstatic to see him. I made a dinner of baked winter squash and sweet potatoes with salmon on the side. It had been a while since I had cooked a full meal and I found I still could make my way around in a kitchen. The food reflected the different hues of orange and the capturing of summer's sunlight in the form of simple vegetables.

We ate and then went upstairs to the bedroom. This would be the third time that I had made love with Andreas and I began to find that my body was gaining in strength. I was truly feeling the healing prayers from the love making improving my physical stamina. The powerful energies that were brought forth as we made love were integrating into my sexual centers. I was able to match Andreas's powerful thrust for thrust. I did not feel weak or depleted any more but I felt more vitality and youthfulness then I had felt in years. Even through I had done exercise programs daily and physically worked hard, nothing compared to this type of lovemaking that was combined with prayer. A total transformation was taking place and I could feel and see it. Love was a great healer. I would tease Andreas that he was my best-kept beauty secret. People around me that had known me saw this transformation taking place. It was in my body and how I carried myself. It was in the light of my eyes but most of all it was in my heart.

Our lovemaking had tenderness and intensity. It was full of prayer and sometimes hysterical laughter. I truly saw and experienced what Christ was meant when he said "as above, so below."

My spiritual life was finally integrated with my sexuality. There was not any place where God was not present. Allowing the thought of God to be within every act made all the difference. The intense power of sexuality combined with prayer and love had the potential to propel two souls very quickly into God consciousness. But this type of power had been hidden from the masses for centuries. Now it was revealing itself to me through the experience with Andreas, my beloved.

Deep healing was taking place in both of us. Every caress was combined with silent prayer, spoken prayer or the deep quietness of each other's soul. I gained an even deeper understanding of how negative thought forms from past relationships became lodged in our bodies. This Tantric relationship helped remove layers and years of hurt, misunderstandings and rejections through the simple act of loving with prayer. We both began to understand this process more deeply during the course of our lovemaking.

When two people are together what they feel towards each other, especially in long-term relationships, is laid upon their beloved's body. If there exists negative rejection over many years, the body feels this and it becomes a crystallized thought. We carry so many projections of others, we rarely realize when this happens to us. We unknowingly accept these thoughts into our bodies and minds. These thoughts then have their effects. This can result in a poor self-image, lack of confidence or even as physical aches and pains. A loving Tantric relationship can remove these thought forms in a very fast and powerful way. Tantra is not only utilizing a very physical sexuality, it is also coupled with very subtle spiritual perceptions. These subtler energies can help a couple detected hurts and pains from the past. Gentleness, understanding, deep love, prayer, breath and the God force that becomes available during love making can remove the obstacles and deep-seated patterns of the past.

Through the different spiritual practices I had engaged in over the years I could experience the spiritual power enter my body. This same power now had moved from my upper chakras, [spiritual centers], down into my womb. It was not isolated in my womb but also freely moved up through the rest of my body out the top of my head and rising into spiritual consciousness above my body like a shaft of light.

I especially experienced this making love to Andreas in a chair the next morning. Andreas sat in the chair and my legs straddled his body. We snuggled and he slipped into my yoni. The rocking motion back and forth intensified my orgasm, until this oceanic power traveled down into my womb like I had never felt before. My womb was filled with explosive, cosmic power. Andreas took my hair in his hands, tossing it in the air and started whispering in my ear "be free, be free." As the rocking back and forth intensified, this power moved up my body and out the top of my head and I began to fly. A wildness was set free in me and it took wings. The sensation of flying through the air was very real as I rocked back and forth with Andreas's lingam deep inside of me. Images raced through the screen of my mind and I saw pagan rites deep in the forest, where women were riding men in the sexual position of woman on top. This image changed to the witch riding the broomstick through the air. I became the witch and my beloved was my steed. I began to understand these pagan sexual rites and the wild orgasmic freedom of flying. The propelling factor was the virility and the power of Andreas's lingam. This experience was totally liberating, throughout the deepest parts of myself.

A few days later I was looking through my book on 'Woman's Myths and Secrets' by Barbara Walker and I looked up the history of the broomstick. The symbol of the broomstick signified a Tantric type of sexual union. Throughout medieval Europe jumping the broomstick was a form of the marriage ceremony outside the Church laws. Understanding started to dawn why the patriarch forbade this sexual position in the church. It was a powerful position for the woman and it gave her the ability to be launched into a freedom of spirit that was totally unacceptable to the church hierarchy. To keep the soul bound and sexuality repressed, this type of cosmic power would be unavailable to the masses. For centuries during the medieval period the missionary position was the only sexual position allowed in marriage, according to church laws.

Even though I had used the woman on top position frequently in past relationships, it did not propel me into this type of experience. The Tantric connection between Andreas and myself had been established in other life times and was being unveiled by our coming together again. It was the sexual alchemy between us that gave us the experiences.

In other situations I would find myself making love to Andreas and just at the peak of orgasm I would rise out of my body and connect with the shaft of light. Automatically my arms would rise and form the shape of the crescent moon. The power would descend and fill me with cosmic energy. I became an empty vessel that the Holy Spirit could fill. I would let myself be filled with this power that was overflowing. When I could not hold anymore I would bring down this power and lay hands on my beloved with prayers for healing and upliftment. At this point Andreas would become totally surrendered and would be receptive to the feminine power that was being funneled through me. Then it was his turn to shake and shimmy like a fish out of water. The power jolted through his body like bolts of lightening from heaven.

This particular position brought about many past life memories. I began to receive understanding of the archetype of Isis, the Egyptian Goddess. This same position let me to experience the opposite of the crescent moon. I was on top of Andreas and at the point of orgasm I felt a huge ball of energy in my hands like a blazing sun. My arms would rise to push upwards this golden disk of light and it would ascend and be released above me into the atmosphere. This reminded me of Egyptian artifacts, with the drawings of Isis holding the golden disk over her head.

The flying feeling would reoccur during this sexual position but instead of flying on a broomstick, my arms would be outstretched behind me with wings like an angel. It felt and appeared much like the Egyptian pictures of the winged goddess. Tantric union in the woman-on-top position unleashed my own inner wildness but also revealed ancient records of Goddess wisdom that was only found in artifacts and fragments of history. My inner sexual life was becoming a living mythos.

CHAPTER 17

# The Tantric Seal

The weeks passed and I was beginning to see Andreas every weekend. It seemed we could not get enough of each other. I began to have problems with being so sexual opened. I would come back from having a beautiful weekend with him and I started to notice I was attracting all kinds of men around me. It was like bees to honey. The sexual openness I was experiencing left me feeling vulnerable.

I had a ridiculous incident at the pizza parlor one evening that my teenage son witnessed; he could not believe his eyes. I was standing in line to order and the man next to me became so excited in my presence that he was literally doing a little dance around me, like a rooster in the barn yard. He was totally unconsciousness of his actions. I just stood there, holding my ground watching him react to my presence. Before this Tantric opening I could walk around, barely being noticed by the opposite sex. Now it had become a problem. I was uncomfortable with so much male sexuality directed towards me. I needed to do something as it was creating sexual confusion.

It was the next weekend with Andreas and Sunday morning had arrived. The weekend was filled with lovemaking and in a few hours I would have to leave for the city. I told Andreas my dilemma of going back out into the world, being so open sexually.

Andreas always had prayed over me for my protection from the beginning of our meeting. Many times he would invoke the Warrior Buddhas to surround me. The Warrior Buddhas are the protectors of the Dharma. They have a very wrathful and fiery aspect. Their faces often look very fierce and scary. They are portrayed this way to scare away anything that could harm you. Their spiritual office is to protect. I have always emphasized spiritual protection but now I was being introduced to very powerful deities. Their divine office was protection. Since I can remember I have been psychically sensitive. It is very common for me to feel the pain of others and at times even know what people are thinking. This can be a gift but also a curse for one needs to have the ability to discriminate which thoughts and feelings belong to whom. Thoughts at times can run through me that are not at all mine, but belong to those around me. It has taken me years to know the difference and I must admit that I still need to sharpen my tools of discrimination. Invocations of the Buddhas were so effective, it gave me a type of protection that I had never known. But I still seemed very sexually open and I wanted the sexual male attention to stop.

We were in bed and just had finished making love and it was time for me to get dressed and leave. I said to Andreas, "Don't send me out there again without being sealed." I did not even know what I was asking for but those were the words that came out of my mouth. Andreas put his hand at the opening of my yoni and gently cupped me with his palm. The other hand he placed at the crown of my head. He began to call the power down by invoking the Tantric Buddhas, whose particular office is sexual healing and the sexual mysteries. He repeated the words again that we used so often, "I give you my body, heart, soul, and hands." When he felt their presence in him he began to say his request. "Seal my beloved, put her into the Tantric seal of protection that she is seen where she needs to be seen and is invisible where she needs to be invisible." He brought his hand from my yoni up to each Chakra of my body repeating the words "I seal my beloved with the Tantric Seal of Protection." He repeated this six times until he came up to my crown and repeated the Seal of Protection again.

I drove home that night feeling different than just being sur-rounded by the Warrior Buddhas' protection. I now felt like my sexuality was also protected. What I was experiencing with my beloved was very sacred and the last thing I needed to come into my auric field was any man's everyday sexuality. There was a big difference in the two worlds and I did not want the psychic pollution of strangers' projections on the street. I found that the Tantric sealing worked and I was not having the invading male experiences as I had before.

The Tantric union between the Shakta and his Shakti is filled with such spiritually powerful energies that many times in the love making sessions both the male and female are merging with Buddha Presences. Many times I felt like a hollow reed or an empty vessel that the spirit was blowing through.

There is a particular flavor of energy between Andreas and I when we make love. I have no words to explain it, but when we are engaged with each other sexually, this feeling is between us. I can refer to this as our Tantric Connection. It feels so good that it becomes easy and safe to totally surrender to the essence of who Andreas is spiritually. This energy isn't Andreas and it isn't me, but it is the blending of both of us spiritually and it feels absolutely delicious.

Together we started to interact with other people. At one point I had been communicating with a man that I had not at all felt any sexuality with, but was open and friendly. We had been sharing spiritual concepts in our discussions.

During this time I noticed that Andreas's and my sexuality had changed. The feeling that I so often looked forward to when we made love had disappeared. Somehow the Tantric connection was not as strong as I had experienced it before. I didn't know why. I thought maybe he was tired of me. This went on for two week and at one point I felt so bad about the loss, I went to sleep in the other bedroom. I wanted to be alone and try to understand what had happened. The next morning Andreas came in and got me wanting to know what was wrong. We went to our bed and I began to explain what I was experiencing. We started to make love and we invoked the Buddhas giving them our bodies, hearts, and souls. Half way through the session I felt an intense pain in my womb and I knew exactly what had happened. I saw that this man had psychically corded into my womb like a dark fishhook. Andreas kept shuttling in and out I told him what I was experiencing and he began to pray for the removal of this particular man's energy. The pain ceased and I felt the cord release and be removed. This was a very intense experience that left me exhausted afterwards. We both began to understand that this man's cording into me, whether conscious or unconscious, had an effect. This man's desire had clouded our Tantric connection. Now his influence was gone and our Tantric connection was back in tact.

Some of my previous work had been with women, removing psychic hooks from past relationships. When I was doing this type of work I realized how past sexual relationships created barriers in the way of experiencing deep intimacy in present relationships. Now I also realized this could even happen on subtler planes with just thoughts or projection of others. Now imagine the psychic cording and entanglement on subtle sexual planes if a person is having multiple relationships or secret affairs. Astrally it would look like a lot of dark hooks and entangled knots. Many people wonder why they cannot find or have love. Yet with this type of astral garbage in the way, deep intimacy is almost impossible. I am not here to cast judgment on anyone. I know that I have had many experiences being on both sides of the fence and from those experiences I hope that I have extracted some womb wisdom. Unfortunately, this extraction had often taken place the hard way. At this point in time I feel to have a sacred relationship in the dimension that I am speaking from, having multiple sexual partners is out of the question. It diminishes the Tantric circuit between the Shakta and Shakti.

The Tantric connection is developed on the subtle spiritual planes. It represents the blending of two souls. Sacred Sexuality alone is not enough by itself. It is absolutely necessary to be joined with meditation practice. The intuitive knowledge that is cultivated through meditation gives the Tantrikas the wisdom to incorporate and work with the powerful God Force that is being developed during the Tantric union. Right meditation brings the clarity of mind to detect and clear away outside influences that may hinder the two souls.

Today the number of people working in the healing arts is higher than ever before. Massage practice has become popular. Laying-on-of-hands, psychics, crystal gazers...—you name it, it's out there. If the healer does not take the time to clear out other people's subtler energies and problems, becoming psychically overburdened will be the result. The practice of Meditation and clearing techniques become a very important part of any good healer's foundation for healing. The true healing is really just God Power coming through the vehicle. The more a person can dissolve into the Divine, the more healing energies become available. Then all concepts and notions of being a healer, a Tantrika, or a spiritual teacher will fall away. This merging into the Divine is done through daily meditation and prayer.

CHAPTER 18

# Peaking through the Veils of Time

Creating herbal baths has been a favorite pastime of mine for years. I found that bathing in herbs, flowers, and sweet scented oils could transform tensions, release aches and pains and create a sensual mode. I would start out one of these bathes in the kitchen by boiling fresh spring water in a big pot. After the water comes to a boil I would throw in handfuls of herbs and flowers. Many of these plants I collect myself in the fields here in Mt. Shasta where they have absorbed the fresh mountain air, been watered by melted snow and have grown in high altitude climates. I never boil the fragile plants but take the pot off the heat and let them steep well over one hour. Handfuls of roses and calendula would be added from the garden. Sweet white and red clover from the field also can be added to the pot. High Mountain Pennyroyal gathered in alpine meadows with spearmint from the stream beds are popped in the sweet brew. The end result would be a wildflower soup that I would pour into the tub.

I was preparing one of these baths one summer evening for Andreas. I began to set the atmosphere in the bathroom by lighting candles all around the tub. I strained the wildflower soup into the tub and then gathered all the herbs into a washcloth, tied up the four corners to keep the herbs in place. I added a cup of Epsom salt and a few drops of lavender and rosemary oil. The final touch was fresh garden roses floating on top of the bathwater. I went to the kitchen and got a little silver pitcher that I liked to use to pour water from. I guess that was my Aquarius nature coming out. I slipped into my silk kimono and then took Andreas by the hand and invited him into the tub.

Andreas sunk down into the water and I began to slowly pour

the herbal concoction over his body and down his face from my little pitcher. My motions were slow and methodical. The sweet-scented steam surrounded us like a veil of mist in the glimmering candlelight. I pulled his soft red hair back and his face began to change before me. Bleeding through this moment in time was another face from another time ancient and long ago. The Japanese kimono and my own hair slicked back into a tight little bun all seemed too familiar. Memories awakened as I felt we were transferred to a time in Japan when he had been a great warlord and I was his geisha. I scrubbed his back with the sponge and poured water on his skin. Steam, vision, and time seemed to blend together into a timeless, deep love that had continued and never ended. I was there in the past with him and at the same moment here in the present.

I drained the tub and wrapped him in a soft terry cloth towel and then began to rub his body vigorously to bring the blood to the surface of the skin. His skin reddened from the stimulation of the towel. I buried my head into his chest and the subtle fragrance of sweet smelling herbs remained in his red chest hair.

We went to the bedroom and he laid on the bed letting his body release the heat from the bath. I picked up a bottle of massage oil that I had made. It was filled with every flower from the summer garden. I had collected and dried all the garden flowers weeks ago. Later I had placed them into a bottle of almond oil and placed them in the hot summer sun. The garden had become a liquid of flowers and sunbeams. I lavishly poured it on my beloved to soothe his every muscle.

I felt so much love towards this man. This love had a sweetness that I could not contain but would spill over in his presence. I began to have a vision as I worked the oil into his arms and chest. I saw Andreas's life force with no beginning and no end. It was like a golden river of light that had been through many incarnations. I saw many past lives. In some I was with him. In others I was not. The vision changed again and I saw our life forces coming together from the One Source. It was like two rivers that came together and would part and then again would stream back together. The two golden streams were rushing now together to the ocean of God Union. I saw the times that I was not with this soul and a deep sorrow welled up from within me that I had not been there to bring him comfort. A love so deep came surging through my touch as I laid hands upon my Beloved's body. The deepest compassion came out of me towards Andreas and flowed over like water from a fountain. This love began to fill all the lifetimes and spaces that I hadn't been there for him. Never had I experienced such depth with another soul. My heart's love was stretched out beyond time to the one who lay before me. I curled up into his arms. Together we fell asleep.

CHAPTER 19

# Surrender to the Beloved

Weeks passed into months and my experiences and meditations with Andreas became incorporated into my being. My body became used to these new and powerful energies and I adapted to the experiences with more peace and grace. A blending had taken place and what emerged from our being together introduced new spiritual facets in both of our lives.

When I came to visit Andreas we would start by meditating together. My meditations with him let me touch the very essence of who he was for me. I truly began to understand why the eastern custom bowed to the Buddha within another person. This feeling did not come from an outside courteousness but was a sense of feeling the essence of who was before me. This type of surrender happened during one of our nightly meditations.

We were sitting together facing each other in meditation. Usually when I begin to meditate I feel a shaft of light over my head, which I rise into spiritually. To me this light is the God, the Christ, and the Power that is my guiding light. It has many names but is the one source of everyone. I began to silently pray and surrender my life and my entire being to God's greater will. My inner prayers kept expanding to another level of surrender inside of myself. I rose even higher into this shaft of light that I was bathing in. Every breath became another level of surrender. All thoughts ceased, and suddenly I saw the shaft of light go from high above my body into the body of Andreas and come through his heart. The light shone through Andreas's heart and reached out into my heart claiming me spiritually. That evening I knew that I was meant to be with this man. Without a thought my body bowed at his feet and acknowledged the God Essence within him.

### The Sacred Marriage
Your touch is grace to my body.
Your glance is light to my soul.
Your heart beat echoes in the inner chambers of my own heart.
Your breath is your life force blending with mine.
Your passion lights the flame of Divine love within me.
Your kisses are like nectar from the sweetness of flowers.
Your lingam is the power of God's force
entering my sacred chamber.
You are my sweetness, pleasure and greatest treasure here on earth.
With you in my life the significance of every moment is revealed and
amplified a million fold.

We sat together at the altar both on our own meditation pillows; we both entered deeper into the silence. Visions began to unfold in my mind's eye. My appearance began to change. My hair was just as dark but thicker. It was shiny, in a very long braid with jasmine flowers entwined into the folds of the braid. My skin was brown and I was dressed in a bronze sari with a short mid belly length blouse that was trimmed in golden embroidery. I was lavishly decorated with gold bracelets. A ruby stud was set into my nose. Priceless jewels of all kinds adorned and decorated my body.

I was in India at a Tantric temple that I only heard about. I stared at the temple carvings of gods and goddesses entwined into different love making positions. There was a river before me. I began to pray and wash my feet at the river's edge.

Andreas sat before me, his chest bare. The light appeared soft, defused and dreamy. An Indian master stood at our side. He wore a light woolen robe and fleece hat. The aura of the master engulfed both of us with his powerful presence. A bowl of ghee (clarified butter) appeared in my hands and I began to offer it to Andreas and pour it over his head. I was marked with a red dot on my third eye. I took golden saffron from a small bowl beside me and marked Andreas's third eye and then his heart.

I began to take all my jewels and gold bracelets off and I placed them in Andreas's lap. I began to remove my clothing, folding it neatly and placing it into Andreas's hands. Then I sat naked before him only wrapped in my white cotton prayer shawl. I felt my naked body wrapped in the prayers held within the shawl. I began to see the Indian master weave our energies together as if he was performing a wedding ceremony. I felt him blessing our union and showering the secrets of sacred sexuality upon us.

I opened my eyes from the meditation and I saw Andreas before me in deep silence. I crawled into his lap and wrapped my prayer shawl around us and sweetly kissed him.

That night I fell asleep in Andreas's arms. I had a dream that a white bridal veil was thrown at me. The crown of the veil was made of Lily of the Valley. I knew that this is Andreas's favorite flower. The fragrance of the flowers was heavenly. I thought to myself in the dream, oh sometimes they call this flower "Our Lady's Tears." I heard a voice in the dream saying, "Our Lady's Tears are tears for joy."

The ringing of the phone awakened me from my sleep. I answered the phone and someone on the other side of the line enquired if I was Mrs. Mamet. I felt that this meditation and dream indicated the spiritual marriage that had taken place in another dimension of time and space.

CHAPTER 20

# Bed Time Dharma Talks

It was a weekend in Mill Valley and Andreas had come down from Shasta to visit me. We were sitting on my four-poster bed, settling into meditation. The meditation was completed and we snuggled under the covers and began to converse about our different understandings of religious points of view. These dharma talks would naturally arise from different meditation events. Our blending together created understandings for both the Eastern and Western point of view. Our bedroom was where the East truly met the West.

Many times our meditations together would begin with an invocation of the different aspects of various Buddhas or Christ. For some people I know working with both Buddha and Christ would be a contradiction. But Andreas and myself have blended the understanding of the East and the West. Some may say that there is no God in true Buddhism. Buddha introduced the understanding of the discerning mind that enables one to cut through the illusions of the world. When Buddha was asked if there was a God he responded only with his Silence. This Silence was vibrantly alive—it was the answer. Christ on the other hand brought compassion, forgiveness and the understanding of the heart. Both in their own way reached total enlightenment and became that deep silence. Some may say there is no God, just silence. Others may say there is a God. God is that silence taking form. When we merge and surrender to that silence we become the hands and feet of the Divine. The Spirit needs the form to manifest through. Without form there is no manifestation of God or Goddess.

Mankind now lives in a particular time in history that allows instant communication. Through the computer and the Internet we now have access to all kinds of information that has never been available before. The Internet has become a message board for so many types of religions and spiritual points of view that we can surf the teachings of Buddhism, Christianity, Paganism, all in a matter of minutes.

We see so much division and contradiction between various religions. But if we look deeper, we find threads of truth in all of them. One day in meditation I heard "there are as many ways to God as there are people." In that moment I understood the meaning of the statement "for each person must come to the door of his or her own soul to enter and find God's Silence." Religions can bring keys and understanding to do this. However, they also can bring hindrances that keep a soul in the bondage of dogmas that have been twisted and turned into religion for the sake of controlling the masses. The point I am trying to make is that each individual needs to sift through the different religious doctrines and extract the nectar for him or herself. However, I do not suggest engaging in superficial contact with various religious avenues. What I do wish to emphasize is that essential spiritual truth does not change and there are gems of truth on every path. A soul needs to plunge into the depth of spirituality by building a spiritual foundation. That foundation is built through years of practice of meditation and prayer that is effective in bringing realization of the Divine. Many years of commitment and dedication to daily practice are an absolute necessity. It is not enough to go to a church or temple once a week or once a month. Dedication and right meditation and prayer is the key to realization.

For myself reincarnation is a reality. The memory of different embodiments has created for me a harmonious synthesis of many different religious points of views. Our time in history will create for many old souls an experience of completion, assimilating and integrating different religious points of view. It is my hope that the polar opposition between Christians and Pagans can be melded into understanding and tolerance. That the gap between Buddhists and Christians be bridged by compassion. It is my wish that the conflicts between Jew and Moslem be healed by the all-encompassing kindness that resides at the core of each religion. And furthermore I wish to see the arising of wisdom in Christianity that realizes that aboriginal-based spirituality has its own deep insights into the laws of this universe.

The only way to ever heal these divisions is by cleaning out the false doctrines in the various religions that restrict our freedom and our right for spiritual self-determination. Personal spiritual experience needs to be respected. A religious approach that suggests that it is the only one, containing the sole true answers ... needs to be reviewed and subjected to intelligent discrimination.

To heal and mend all the long-standing religious differences a large dose of forgiveness needs to be served up on the plates of the various religions. Even a larger helping of the understanding of one Divine Source in a myriad of different aspects—needs to be digested.

This healing, however, will not happen as long as any religion holds on to the belief of being the one true religion. It will remain distant as long as the Native Americans or Pagans hold on to the anger for being persecuted for practicing their religions. Harmony will remain a faraway dream if Muslims, Jews and Christians choose hate above forgiveness.

What I am proposing is not simple, but can begin to happen within each individual. As individuals we need to heal the self-importance, prejudice or anger that lives with in each one of us. Forgiveness is the key to World Peace. As individuals activate forgiveness in their lives for the wrongs that have happened to them personally, then forgiveness can begin to happen on a greater scale among religions and even nations. This will bring about new possibilities during an age that will flood us with information that has not ever been available before.

Every religion or spiritual path seems to contain aspects that simultaneously empower and disempower. The blessing of Buddhism is the practice of awareness every second of one's life. On the other hand there exists the neurosis that arose as a consequence to the interpretation of Shakyamuni Buddha's statement "All life is suffering." The resulting illness of Buddhism is that it can negate life. The Buddhist concept of detachment has been swallowed by the fear of living life itself. It is through fully living that detachment can be obtained.

Hinduism, while having contributed the blessing of powerful and effective yogic techniques and meditations, has also polluted this planet with the introduction of the cast system, that require a Brahman to cleanse himself if so much as a shadow of an untouchable was cast upon his body.

Christianity's blessings are its mystical traditions that allow the seeker to have the living experience of Christ. The neurosis of Christianity is to believe that it is the one true faith and everyone is a sinner. This mindset of being the sinner never leaves a soul feeling worthy to receive God.

The beauty of Islam is the utter devotion and longing for Allah. This is especially expressed in the mystic core of Sufism. Islam's personal disease is its radical readiness to die in a holy jihad for a cause that will make the believer a Martyr, to be reborn in a paradise where all needs are lavishly met. Additionally, no other religion has gone as far in repressing the female population as has Islam.

The positive aspects of the New Age movement can be seen in its ability to embrace and assimilate many different spiritual paths and see the oneness of them all. The New Age's negative side lies in its inability for long-held discipline and effort. Due to its potential lack of one-pointedness it may not reach the depth of discipline-based tradition, leaving the seeker disempowered and without substantial foundation.

The wonderful aspect of Tantra lies in its ability to accept, celebrate and transform all aspects of life into Divine Experience. Tantra, however, is direly misunderstood and falsely interpreted when the Tantric concepts are used as an excuse to engage in indiscriminate excess, be it sexual or other. Tantra in it highest form embraces every aspect of life but what needs to be remembered is personal responsibility and the fact that every action is associated with its respective price. This fact requires emphasized attention in the Tantric domain—it is often forgotten. The power of discrimination is a necessary key to the Tantric path.

The paths of Shamanism reflected in Native American Teachings and European Paganism engender respect for the living spirit within all of nature. This is very much needed to preserve and restore the planet that we all live on during this time in history. The negative aspect of this path of power is revealed when individuals are attracted to personal power not balanced by love and wisdom. The teachings can turn into a misuse of power for selfish, personal gain. In both of these paths group anger is often expressed because of the annihilation from the Inquisition and Genocide. This can leave an individual soul bound in the polarity of duality. It is through accelerating the flow of divine forgiveness that freedom from the past can be achieved. This type of karmic debt can only be balanced by standing in our own truth and not letting the hooks of duality set us back into experiences that continue to recreate past events. This does not mean that these injustices should go unnoticed or not given voice. However, the pit falls of anger need to be transformed.

Last and not least, the feminine face of God needs to be recognized and honored in all religions and all paths to restore balance in this world. Women need to be recognized for their own wisdom and spiritual insight in all religions. They need to be given a respected place within the religious structures.

CHAPTER 21

# The Christos

The next morning we woke up and had our morning coffee in bed. Then we settled down into another meditation. As we sat on the bed in meditation, Andreas began to invoke Christ presence. I sat in silence with my eyes closed. *The visions started to come in view, as I rose in consciousness I saw the living Christ on his throne, his dark hair streaming downward. A crown of jewels graced his brow and light appeared as a downpour in a perfect alignment with Andreas's body. Andreas seemed to melt and all that was left was a cross of Golden Light in front of me.*

*Appearing from behind me, in a horizontal light beam, I saw the Lineage of Mariam, Mother Mary, the Magdalene, Saint Ann and Saint Elizabeth. All of a sudden they began to blend into different faces of the Goddess from ancient times. These were the spiritual women who had walked the Path of the Divine Mother. This lineage appeared behind me and then went straight through the center of my heart and entered into the heart of Andreas. It was light meeting light from a vertical plane, joining the light on a horizontal plane.* All I could do in the moment was honor the vision and bow my head to the one before me in Christ, through Christ, in love through love. Our bodies became Christ's Body. Our hearts were the heart of the Christos. Our souls lay upon the Altar of the Most High. Love could be performed in every act of passion that was fueled by God's love and God's grace. Every caress became the hand of the Divine. Every kiss was the kiss of the Beloved. The banquet table was laid before us. Our bodies became the bread. Our love became the wine and our ecstasy was Holy Communion that entered into our lovemaking.

Christ himself was born from the womb and entered the world of humankind. How can it not be pure? To invoke the Power of Christ in the beginning of love making is a way to heal the split between sexuality and spirituality. To let ourselves rise in consciousness during the sexual act can awaken the dormant Serpent Power (Kundalini) and thus enable us to see the face of the Divine in the Beloved.

The Divine called forth in the simple act of lovemaking can bring healing beyond what the mind can comprehend. It is time to bring God into the bedroom. God has always been there anyway. Our minds just shut out the presence of God. This then resulted in the lack of love and consciousness in the sexual act. It is easy to look out upon the world and see the distortion of sex without God. Once the Holy Spirit is invited in without shame, knowing God is there anyway, love, healing and ecstasy beyond human limitations can take place. I am experiencing this over and over again with my Beloved.

To quote scriptures without experience or true understanding is not the deeper knowing. But once one has experienced the presence of God, the need for all arguments disappears. One does not need to be convinced in theory of God's existence. One has entered the knowing and that knowing becomes our truth and our reality.

Once God is experienced in the sexual act and the realization arises that there is no separation, lovemaking becomes a prayer and a divine act of God and Goddess. This can only be experienced, not taught. It is through the grace of the experience that one will know this truth. All separation of spirit and sexuality, all shame and guilt will fall away. It will disappear like darkness, dispelled from a room after the light has been switched on. God is there, Goddess is there.

A body that is properly loved shortens the spirit's journey to the Divine. If you find and enter the gate of cherishing, the whole world of Tantra will unfold as a simple and natural by-product.

We began to make love after the Christos vision. Andreas lay on top of me and with his feet he gently pushed my own feet into a position of being tightly wrapped and crossed at the ankles. I was lying in a Christ-like position across the bed as we made love. The energy surged upward from my lower Chakra, exploding in my heart. My arms were stretched out over the bed like being on the cross. My heart was opening like it never had been opened before. Deeper I dove into this Divine love. I saw Christ coming to me in a white robe with open arms. I was orgasmic as explosion after explosion burst in my heart. The passion of Andreas melted into the vision and the experience of Christ. There was no higher and no lower. All separation of the two melted into the pure love of the experience. Andreas was making love. I was making love and Christ was the center of our love. Let Thy Kingdom Come in every act.

CHAPTER 22

# Allowing Beauty

Andreas is the contemplative type. Many hours of meditation and self-reflection gave him interesting insights into how people function. It was one of those bedtime conversations when the issue of beauty arose. Andreas would tell me how my beauty nourished him. He went on to share that it was my inner beauty that fed his soul. Even though he appreciated the package of my human vehicle, one always can use some nice curves to hang onto, he explained. But it is the inner beauty that needs cultivation and without this a person can fall into all the outside trappings of beauty, devoid of content. Beauty without content ultimately leads to failure in relationships. The media have projected upon society the standards of beauty, which are ever-changing and have left many psychological scars in those of us who failed to live up to the media-projected standards. You can witness this in women's eating disorders and preoccupation with cosmetic surgery to the point that it becomes life threatening.

Just because you have an incredibly beautiful woman before you and or a beautiful man, that does not guaranty a good relationship or even great sex. Great sex includes the spiritual merging of two souls. In great sex, individuals dissolve and let go of all separateness. It really has nothing to do with breast size or how muscular the body is. When hearts become open and vulnerable, the beloved can then be embraced. The beauty of the beloved's soul brings nourishment so powerful, it easily heals wounds and scars from many of life's experiences. Ultimately, the lover and the beloved dissolve into the divine.

When all repressions are released and dissolved the primal woman or man is honored. Then our love can be expressed without shame and guilt. We can be free in the act of lovemaking. When the separation of body and spirit is dissolved in the human form, then this new-found freedom can express itself in our sexuality.

Sexual repression creates distortion in people. That distortion can manifest in acts of violence, rape and crude pornography. Sexuality without responsibility and discernment can create unwanted children, venereal diseases and unhealthy relationships.

It is through exercising the wisdom of discrimination that we see who is before us. It is that mode that will heal a broken heart and protect from future pain. When we can truly see our partners for who they are, and cease projecting on them what they are not, then we can begin to have a genuine relationship.

Every relationship in this world has a price. Every person we take on in a relationship has good qualities and also flaws. It takes wisdom and mindfulness to read the price tag before purchase. Some packages have a nice wrapper but the price tag is high, either on the emotional, psychological or material level (or all of the levels mentioned).

While love is one of the main ingredients of good relationships, love alone is not enough. Compatibility too needs to be between two souls. Without it, love will be worn away. Seeing the other for who they are and appreciating who they are (without desiring to change) is the ultimate last ingredient of a beautiful relationship. If we love someone but cannot see him/her for who they truly are, ultimately separateness and loneliness will follow because of this lack of understanding. Love, compatibility and seeing the beloved – these are the magic ingredients.

Sexuality expressed through love without repression can become a sacred sacrament. It can be one of the holiest acts for two souls to join in. It can be an act of Divine Celebration.

CHAPTER 23

# Meditations and Mantras

In the summer of 1997 I moved to Mt. Shasta to live with Andreas. This was a major step for me because I was leaving behind my work and my independence. But I knew it was the right thing and I took the leap. It was like coming home for me. Mt. Shasta had been my home for seven years in the seventies. It was wonderful. Life became quieter and simpler. With Andreas's loving support I was able to take the time I needed for my meditations and myself.

Over the months our meditation practice together began to deepen and developed into something new and different. Our meditation room has a view of Mt. Shasta. The spiritual atmosphere that this Holy Mountain emits aids one's spiritual practice. High and holy mountains have traditionally been used in many religions for retreats and hermitages. The natural beauty and silence of mountainous areas seems conducive to spiritual growth.

Andreas is a treasure trove of Eastern meditation practices. It was because of the profound experiences I had with him that my spiritual direction began to change again, moving into Eastern meditation practices. It felt like I was coming home. In the beginnings of my spiritual quest in my early twenties I had a choice of going into an Eastern direction but because of the Sanskrit language I took another path, as languages have always been difficult for my dyslexic mind to comprehend. Andreas was patient with me. He slowly began to teach me the Eastern words and their meanings.

Most of our practices stemmed from both Buddhism and Hinduism, but at the same time something entirely new was created. Our meditations became a hybrid of Eastern thought that we adapted for the Western mind. We began to also use the modern technology in the form of listening to Sacred Chants on CD Players.

We both love mantra work (Chanting sacred names of God). Mantra practice is found in Buddhism and Hinduism. Even the Hail Mary found in Catholicism is a form of mantric prayer. Each mantra invokes a spiritual vibration that is connected to the Divine or a certain aspect of the Divine. When you recite a mantra you can connect yourself with all the sages and yogis that have ever said this mantra before you. There are mantras for healing, for wisdom, spiritual creativity, the list is endless. To establish a mantric practice, traditionally the mantra is done everyday for forty days. The least number of mantras repeated should be 108. Our own practice incorporates the mantra repeated many times more then this. Many nights we would sit on our meditation pillows together, chanting one of our favorite mantras for the next forty-five minutes. Then we would end the practice with fifteen or twenty minutes of invocations. We would then end the meditation by sitting silently and absorb what took place.

A wondrous thing began to happen in our high tech world over the last few years. People have started making CDs with many of the ancient mantras. All of a sudden the world had been presented with a beautiful flower from the East. For the first time, Mantras were introduced into the main stream of society. In earlier years one would have to travel to India to receive a mantra from a guru and begin the practice. Of course, this would be the most preferable way since the practitioner would benefit from the blessing of the guru's own mantric practice. Additionally, one would also experience the blessings of all the teachers behind the guru who passed the mantra down though the ages.

However, I have found through personal experience that I have benefited greatly from chanting the CD Mantras even without the direct teaching from the guru. The mantric prayers on CDs too carry with them teachers and sages on the inner planes that are more than willing to bring their blessings to those whose heart is earnest and willing to do the discipline.

Many of the Western spiritual seekers of the 60s and the 70s now have come into their own spiritual flowering and are expressing what they have learned from their gurus in the form of mantric music. Some of the CDs I am referring to are from recording artists like Krishna Das, Henry Marshal, Deva Premal, and the beautiful book and Mantric CD by Thomas Ashley-Farrand. Now instead of sitting by ourselves repeating our mantra we have the added spiritual power of the CD mantras. We would choose a mantra from the CD and set the CD player on repeat. Then we would chant the same mantra for an extended period of time. It was amazing what it did to for our meditations.

One evening Andreas came upstairs and did the Gayatri Mantra for two hours straight with Deva Premal's CD, Essence. This Gayatri mantra is known as one of the most ancient of all Sanskrit Mantras.

Om bhur bhuvah swah
Tat savitur varenyam
Bhargo devasya dhimahi
Dhiyo yo nah pra chodayat

I have seen many different translations for this mantra but I will use the one that Deva Premal used on her Essence CD:
"Through the coming, going, and the balance of life
The essential nature that illumines existence is the adored one.
May all perceive through subtle intellect the brilliance of enlightenment."
Quote from Deva Premal's CD "Essence"

Andreas finished his meditation and I went upstairs to go to bed and I turned off the light. I was alone in the bedroom/meditation room. The whole room was lit up. Even though the room was physically dark, it was filled with a golden light. I realized the chanting of this mantra had created the light. It was truly an amazing experience with tangible results. A few months later Andreas and I met Deva Premal at one of her workshops. Premal and her partner Miten began to tell us what happened to them when recording this mantra for the CD. They had a very similar experience happening to them: the room being filled with light after a couple of hours of recording.

Many early mornings I have gotten up before sunrise to build a small fire and sing the Gayatri mantra to the early morning sunrise. Traditionally this was the way it had been done for centuries. After doing this mantra for a time I began to see on the inner realm old yogis and sadhus being with me every time I built the fire and sang the mantra. This vision of the yogis affirmed for me how the lineage of the mantra is accessed and carried when you practice the mantra daily.

CHAPTER 24

# Embodying the Buddhas

Over the months Andreas and I experienced a deepening of love for each other and our shared loved for the Divine. Meditation was even more a part of our relationship than our sexuality. Invocation of the different presences of various Buddhas is part of the daily fabric of our life together. During our meditations, I would experience different aspects of the divine as we called forth and merged with the enlightened ones. A Buddha is one who has achieved enlightenment. This does not stop with those who became fully awakened in the East. Enlightened ones existed in all religions and nationalities. They can be either female or male. There are so many wise ones behind the veil of time and space to assist and help us if we would only ask. There are so many divine aspects and offices in the infinite realm of God/dess.

Truly, the Buddhas are awakened souls who have dissolved their human identities and merged into the Divine. The invocations are not just a repetition of words. Through daily discipline one can literally begin to feel different aspects of Divine Presence as we invite the Divine to accompany us in our meditation or even in our sexuality. The different graces and qualities of each Buddha would pour and shower into our bodies, filling us with a very unique presence. This is such a exhilarating experience for the body and heart and a tremendous nourishment for the soul.

I experienced the invocation of Kuan Yin as engulfing me in a gentle peace, accompanied by a pink radiant light. When I call the Warrior Buddhas, the protectors of the dharma, they enter my body like fiery marching soldiers, armed with armor and swords to cut through any of my obstacles. At other times I would experience their presence as a spinning wheel of fire that would whirl around my body as a protective shield.

The calling of Jesus Christos brings the descending of a golden silence that unfolds inside of me with the sweetness of compassion. When I invoke the Divine Mother Mary, she brings motherly comfort and protection. Invoking the Tantric Buddhas before lovemaking reveals many of the secrets of sacred sexuality and can only be explained through the experience.

Many of the great spiritual traditions have their different spiritual pantheons that have been prayed to for Divine guidance. Underlying all these apparent differences, there exists Divine Reality, inviting us to drop the illusion of separation in the realization that many paths lead to the same Divine Home.

Behind the illusion of separation, Buddhists, Christians, Muslims, Jews, Pagans and Aborigines can co-exist without strife. True enlightenment dissolves all separation into the Silence of the Void. Forms change, religions rise and fall and blend into one another over centuries of time. The Divine has expressed itself through many forms. The separation of those forms only exists in the minds of man. It is time to enter into the heart of humanity and dissolve the separation created by religious dogmas. The emptiness is what all forms of the Divine are born out of and are returning to. Just as a wagon wheel has many spokes to the central hub of the wheel, the center is still. Even as the wheel turns the hub of the wheel remains motionless. Different religious approaches are like the spokes of the wheel that bring us to the spiritual center. When a soul makes the big jump into the void, then all religions and all self-identifications disappear.

CHAPTER 25

# Candlelight and Cathedrals

We planned a trip to Europe together to visit Andreas's mom and also had a few days to stop over in Paris. There was a lot of planning before the trip but one of my main concerns was not to break my mantric practice. I was in the middle of a forty day practice and I decided to pack two mini CD players with headphones with my mantra CDs. Airplane flights often come with delays and we found ourselves waiting in the airport. I put a mantra CD into my player, put my headphones on and sat back listening to a chant. This particular mantra was called Dhanyavad. The mantra is said to bring joy, gratitude, and forgiveness.

I sat there in my chair watching all humanity walking by as I was repeating this mantra silently in my mind with the CD. I began to see the face of the Divine in all the people before me, tears of joy streamed down my face. An overwhelming love welled up in my heart for all those who walked passed me. I was sitting right there in the middle of San Francisco's International Airport, swimming in an ocean of love. This gave me a whole new perception of waiting for airplanes.

This was my first time in France. Andreas speaks French, which made our traveling though the city smooth. We arrived at our hotel in Paris, which had a beautiful view of the Eiffel Tower. My excitement was overwhelming. I wanted to see everything at once. But my first wish was to go to the oldest church of Paris, St. Germain-des-Pres and light a candle. Since we were staying next to the Eiffel Tower we decided to walk along the River Seine to St. Germain. The very first signs of spring were beginning to show as blossoms began to bud on the trees. We walked past the Eiffel Tower, admiring the architecture but not stopping. There was a sea of tourists to swim through, and I had other priorities at the moment. We walked down the banks of the River Seine witnessing some of the most beautiful statues and architecture in the World.

We came upon a bridge with a statue of Mars, whose body reminded me of Andreas, naked. I teased him that he must have been the model for this sculpture.

Everyone walks in Paris. It is easy to see why since there is so much for the senses to experience. The aromas that waft from the Bistros are whetting the appetite as we walk by. The golden statues that overlook the city streets from their high and lofty positions glimmer in the afternoon sunlight. You can see delicate lace curtains peeping from the windows of Parisian apartment buildings. Women are gracefully walking down the street with their cashmere scarves neatly wrapped around their necks with the faint smell of fine perfume, which leaves a trail behind them.

We arrived in St. Germain, which is filled with sidewalk cafes, movie theaters, publishing houses, and interior designers. But I was looking for the Church of St. Germain, and after asking several people for directions, we finally found it. This basilica originated in 542. It was the first Gothic building of Paris, but over the centuries of remodeling, it also has been given Romanesque arches and 6th century marble columns.

We walked into the church. I have found that in Cathedrals it wasn't the main altar that necessarily had the spiritual juice but the small altars that are built at the sides of the church. This is where people would go to have a private prayer with their favorite saint. Centuries upon centuries of prayers would build a vortex of spiritual nourishment. I found a small alcove that had an altar to St. Theresa, the Little Flower. I knelt before her since she was one of my favorite childhood saints. I lit a candle before her feet and as I struck the match I went into deep prayer. A beautiful voice arose inside the cathedral, singing praises to Mary in French. My spirit began to soar with the sweetness of the singing woman's voice. Electric energy began to move though my body like a bolt of lightening. I became a current of electricity, opening my arms wide so that this energy could pass though me. The voice sang in even higher octaves as the Divine embraced me completely at that moment. An inner voice arose in me saying the words "Welcome home, my daughter." Now I felt I had arrived in Paris! The singing subsided, and I began to come back into a quieter state inside my body.

We left the church but before leaving I saw an old man on the steps, panhandling. I placed some Francs in his can and we walked across the avenue to a sidewalk cafe.

CHAPTER 26

# The City of Lovers

We saw many beautiful sites during our stay in Paris. However, it was not only the sites that left their impressions upon my mind. I was also impressed by the confidence the Parisians displayed. It appeared to both of us that the men and women of Paris have a sexual confidence that we did not see in America as much. This confidence did not have anything to do with how a person looked for we saw this same self-reliance in people of all ages, all sizes, beautiful and not so beautiful—it was still there. Many of the women's faces I saw had a sensual satisfaction that quietly resided under the surface. We began to ask ourselves why that was.

Our first lunch in Paris was at the Hilton Hotel. The tables were placed very close to each other. One could almost rub elbows with the people at the next table. The restaurant was filled with business people. Andreas and I watched quietly the two men next to us having their meals. One of the men was huge, maybe 250 pounds, but it was not his size that impressed us. In spite of his size he was suave. The way he ordered his food, ate his lunch, and wore his suit… everything about him was filled with sexual confidence.

We were in the elevator of our Hotel when an older couple in their late 60s entered. You could look into the woman's face and see sexual satisfaction, as they exchanged glances and kisses in the elevator. This reminded me of something a friend of mine, who is French, had said to me one day during a conversation about relationships. He said they have an old saying in France, "the best soup is made in an old pot." This older couple definitely created a good soup.

Andreas and I began to discuss the differences we saw in the people of Paris compared to those in America. Often I would see a beautiful American woman but I could look into her face and see dissatisfaction. Maybe the process of becoming the independent woman, not needing a man, has cut her off from something very fundamental in human nature: her own sexuality and sensual nature. I see this not so much in the younger American woman, but in the middle-aged woman who has gone through life and has been wounded by love. She has closed herself off from the possibilities of relationship. I see it in the woman who is in a relationship and is not being fed emotionally or sexually in a way that awakens her sensual nature. Often I tell Andreas that he is my best-kept beauty secret. When I am being made love to, it is the afterglow that brings sparkle to my eyes, lightness to my step and even my body holds itself differently.

I realize that not everyone in Paris is in a great relationship or a relationship at all. I began to ask myself what is it that feeds the people that they reflect such self-assurance. One thing is that beauty is everywhere. Everywhere you walk your eyes can feast on exquisite art, sculptures, and architecture. The French food presentation is more like an art form then a regular meal. Even simple open-air markets displayed the vegetables as if arranged by a great artist. Beauty was everywhere. Beauty brings healing. Beauty feeds the soul through the senses. Even the French language sounds like a poetic song if only conveying everyday phrases.

It seemed that it did not matter if a person was young or old, thin or fat, ugly or beautiful: the sensual confidence was present. The Parisians' senses were saturated with sensuality though art, food, fine perfumes, beautiful clothes, and the uninhibited way they have expressing their affection in a relationship.

The American woman, in her striving to gain equality with the man, has at times castrated the American male in the process. Woman's liberation has brought about many needed changes to this country, but in the process, it also has caused a few imbalances. Some of the American women dress the sexy image and then castrate the males that they attract if they express desire for her. I am not talking here about male advances that are truly abusive.

It is interesting to note that in some of the political arenas where women have come forward to condemn men for their alleged sexual advances, they are the first ones to have the face lift and liposuction with the first increase of financial income. What does this say? I want the power of the female seductress but don't look at me and don't touch me. I feel that the media bombards us with the sexy woman's image. However, in the American woman's unconscious mind there are still puritanical values at play.

Hollywood and the media have created an unrealistic image of woman that very few women in this country could ever live up to. We are exposed to billboards, magazines, even ads on the city buses that are reflecting some bigger-than-life sexy woman. No wonder why many American women, even the beautiful ones, cannot accept their bodies just the way they are. There is always the advertising environment that is bombarding us with this perfect image.

I have noticed that some of the magazines are beginning to change this by portraying larger and older women in beautiful fashions. These are the first steps of bringing healing to the mind of American women. The biggest population segment that is buying from the retail market nowadays is the baby boomers. It would be a wise business decision for the media to bring out realistic advertisement for women of this age.

If you have ever taken the time to watch foreign films you might notice that many of the actresses look like everyday people. I have found that both in English and Australian films. The actors have taken on more character roles rather then being bigger-than-life beauty icons. I think that the media are just beginning to address some of these issues.

The baby boomers are now coming of age, and with that age, wisdom begins to dawn as youth begins to fade. Beauty is no more just skin deep, or a size six dress. It is something greater than the surface appearances. The state of mind and the kindness of heart is what feeds the soul's greater beauty. In a woman's youth many doors will be open to her if she is beautiful. But if she has not developed her inner nature time will steal away her looks. When forty-five comes, it is very hard to hide negative thinking or polluted emotions, for the body will reflect what has been hidden underneath the surface. The stressful life can also take its toll in the later years of life. The care and feeding of the Shakti Female Energy will develop beauty. This may come in the form of a loving relationship or getting yourself out of an abusive relationship. Surrounding yourself with art, natural beauty, or a refined lifestyle will feed your Shakti. Meditation is one of the best beauty treatments, for Peace of Mind reflects as a quiet beautiful inner light on any face. Connecting with Spirit adds sparkle to your eyes and a spark to your life. In Paris I saw beauty in an environment that I felt fed those who lived in this city. I witnessed a sexual confidence in the people that did not depend on how they looked physically. It truly is a city for Lovers.

CHAPTER 27

# CD Samadhi

When we arrived in Germany, Andreas's mom showed us to our room, which had been Andreas's room as a child growing up. Being in his childhood room at the home he grew up in stirred my feelings of deep intimacy towards Andreas. It was like entering into a window of his past that had molded him into who he was in the present day.

We sat around the kitchen table visiting with Andreas's mom, drinking rosehip tea and talking about our trip. It was bedtime so we retired to our rooms. After a few hours of sleep jet lag kicked in and we both found ourselves waking up in the middle of the night, not being the least bit sleepy. We put our CD players on, and laid there, holding hands, listening to mantras. We did this for hours, silently repeating our mantras in the stillness of the night.

By the third evening in Germany I decided to go to bed early since Andreas and his mom had a lot of catching up to do and I don't speak German and she doesn't speak English. I lay there with my CD headphones on and plugged into a triple Goddess mantra on the same Henry Marshall CD. This mantra honors Saraswati, Maha Lakshmi, and Durga, the three aspects of the Hindu Goddess. Saraswati represents creativity, Lakshmi abundance and Durga wrathful protection. As I slipped into the chanting of this mantra, something wonderful happened. I laid down in a yogic resting pose called Shavasana, also known as corpse pose. This posture is often used after yoga practice to create a deep relaxation state. You rest on your back with the palms of your hands facing upward, legs together and feet gently flopping out to the sides. As the mantric meditation began to take hold of me, a spiritual energy arose inside myself so profound and deep that I could

143

not even move a little finger. My body became like stone while my mind was in a complete state of bliss as I listened to the mantra. I understood for the first time the deeper meaning of the corpse posture.

The beauty about headphones is that the mantra is actually felt deep inside the body. Every atom becomes filled with the mantric sound. This state of not being able to move lasted for the next few hours. I was not scared at all. I was God-possessed. Total deep relaxation, total God Union, total contentment was all I felt. I slowly started to come back into the movement of my body. I took off my headphones and then Andreas opened the door. He had just finished his visit with his mother. I had my own visit with the Great Mother myself.

CHAPTER 28

# The Honoring of the Female Buddhas

One evening I stopped to think about all the self-realized women who had ever lived. How many of these female Buddhas had walked silently though their lives, never being recognized for their enlightenment. I decided to invoke their Presence.

**I call forth the Power and the Presence of all Female Buddhas from the past, the present and the future, especially those who were never recognized down through the centuries of time.**

I asked that their wisdom be brought forth and given to me so that they could finally have a voice. The Female Buddhas came as nameless ones. Some of them came from the East, while others I saw as temple priestesses from ancient times. This particular invocation became my favorite meditation. After saying this invocation for many months something wonderful happened. It was my first Christmas in Mt. Shasta after moving here. We had invited my mother and father for Christmas Eve and we had just finished dinner and had begun opening presents. My mother handed Andreas and I a package and was very excited for us to open it. Andreas pulled back the Christmas wrapping to reveal a beautiful antique wooden Kuan Yin statue. She had been passed down to my mother from her cousin who had recently passed away. David, my mother's cousin was a very scholarly man but he was an atheist. Oddly enough he had two beautiful possessions that he displayed in his home. One was a beautiful picture of a Madonna and child and the other was this very old Kuan Yin statue. I examined the statue and noticed that on the face of Kuan Yin the dark wood had split, leaving her face scared. Looking deep into the statue's serene face, her scar reminded me of looking at the face of the Black Madonna of Czechoslovakia. This famous Black Madonna is noted for many cures and miracles. But across her face she bears a scar. I now was looking at an Eastern Madonna that bore the same marking naturally from the splitting of the black ebony wood.

A few days later I suggested to Andreas that we should dedicate this statue on the altar since she had never been properly blessed. We put the Kuan Yin on our home altar and started to do the mantra Om Mani Padme Hum, the mantra of Avalokiteshvara, the Buddha of Compassion. This Buddha came to the gateway of his enlightenment, and at the point of being able to pass into Nirvana, he heard the cries of humanity's suffering. He vowed to come back again and again until all of humanity had gained enlightenment. This became the Bodhisattva vow. When Buddhism came to China, Avalokiteshvara transformed into his Feminine aspect, Kuan Yin. In Tibet Avalokiteshvara is known as Chenresig and his female Shakti is Tara. Tara has many different manifestations, but the most popular is Jetsun Dolma, Green Tara, known as the Mother of the Buddhas.

As our Kuan Yin statue stood on the altar with candles flickering around her and the smell of sandalwood incense filling the air, the words Om Mani Padme Hum (The Jewel in the Lotus of the Heart) hummed though my voice and vibrated in my head like a hive of honey bees. Realizations began to take form in my mind as to why this statue had come to me in such a way. Symbolically this statue lived in the house of a person who had no belief in the Divine. So this Female Buddha was in a home where she was not recognized. She bore the scar of the Black Madonna across her face. The Black Madonna is the Feminine Aspect of the Divine that has not been honored, whether this comes in the form of Mother Earth, or Sacred Sexuality, or Female Saints and Shaktis that have not been given a voice in the world religions of the East or the West. I looked at the symbolic meaning of this Kuan Yin statue that was given to Andreas and I and realized she now was being honored. We dedicated her and all Female Buddhas that had never been recognized on the altar that day.

CHAPTER 29

# Eight Years Later

The meeting of Andreas and the experiences that happened to me took me about two and half years to incorporate into my body. We are still together doing our practices, learning our lessons and seeing the Divine peek through the veils of our daily human experiences. Karma can be quickened in these types of relationships since they are based on God Realization that goes beyond the human romantic love that we all have seen in the movies. The goal is to wake each other up and bring forth creations on this earth plane that are both wisdom and compassion based. I can't say that this is always easy, for life always has its ups and downs even in Sacred Relationships. Gaining wisdom often carries a high price. The pearl of perfection is cultivated in human experience. One must learn how to rise above human imperfections and see the Divine and the human braided together as one. We clearly mirror ourselves back to each other, cleaning and clearing patterns and old programming that no longer serve us or humanity. This is the Great Work.

Little by little I hear of sacred couples finding each other. Their love explodes forth and they join together for causes greater then themselves. These are the sacred relationships of the future. Sacred couples become mirrors for each other through love and truth. This alchemy will bring greater inner awareness. This awareness will become a ripple and then a wave bringing us home to the shore of God Realization.

CHAPTER 30

# Meditations

# Womb Healing Meditation

Sit in a chair comfortably, spine straight, legs firmly on the floor. Close your eyes and begin to take a few deep breaths. Visualize that you are breathing through your entire body—not just your lungs. Now see a shining bright star above the top of your head, just a few inches above the center of your head. Right above the first star see another star, shining just as bright. See a third star above the second star and keep doing this, one star after another in straight alignment until you have counted 12 bright shining stars. Allow your consciousness to be hovering high above your body, merging with your Higher Self.

Now take a very deep breath and let a hollow shaft of white light go straight down through the 12 stars and enter into the top of your head. The hollow shaft of light now goes through your brain connecting with your spine. Remember to breathe deeply as you bring the light down through your spine and out your tailbone. Keep breathing deeply. Let the shaft of light go through your chair into the floor beneath your feet. Deep into the earth the shaft of light travels. Visualize the shaft branch out into the ground, thus anchoring the light. Take a few deep breaths. Then send your breaths into the shaft of light. Let it travel from the Higher Self into the earth and back again.

Travel in consciousness to your Crown Chakra. If you cannot see the color of the Chakra, pick the first color that pops up in your mind. Usually the colors chosen are purple, pink or blue. Find a color that is soothing for you. Remember *your* color.

Now it is time to travel to your womb. As you bring your consciousness to your womb, find your ovaries. Go to the right ovary first and feel how it is doing. Is it tight? Are there dark colors around it? Do you see any objects wrapped around it? Do you see or feel hooks in the ovary? Everyone will have a different experience. Here use your own intuition. Remember to also check out the back of the ovary. Now that you can feel the condition of your ovary, we are ready for the cleansing meditation.

So remember the hollow shaft of light in your spine? We are going to use your breath as a vacuum cleaner. You breathe in and suck up all dark colors or bound-up energy from your ovary and bring it to the hollow shaft of light. Then breathe out and let the debris go through the shaft out of your body to the Mother Earth who is the great transformer. As you breathe in and out and clear the accumulated energies around the ovary, pictures or thoughts will come to mind: old boyfriends and husbands. Don't be afraid to see who has attached themselves to your creative power. Look and then sweep them away, clearing your ovary and reclaiming your creative power for yourself. By now you might be feeling a little overwhelmed. Return to normal breathing. Take the color of your choice from your Crown Chakra and use this color like a soothing healing balm upon your ovary. Heal your ovary. Bring soothing and comfort to it. Once you feel a little more soothed start again with the vacuum cleaner breath just as you have done before. If you find a problem or person remaining stubbornly attached to your ovary, visualize a crystal knife removing the person's energy. Keep breathing and move the unwanted thought forms through the hollow shaft of light out of your body into Mother Earth. Remember to also go to the back of the ovary for clearing. It is now time to apply the soothing light. Do this until you feel calm. You are now finished with the right ovary.

Go to the left ovary and repeat the same process that you did with the right ovary. Once the ovaries are completed go to the womb, using the same breathing process. As you go through the ovaries and the womb, thoughts or pictures from your past will arise. Examine the pictures and then release them completely into the hollow shaft, into the earth. Always follow up with the soothing color balm afterwards.

\*\*\*

Once you feel you are done disconnect the bottom of the hollow tube and release it into the earth. Breathe in and let the remaining shaft of light go up through the spine and out your head, back through the 12 stars, breathe out and come back down to your body. Open your eyes and give yourself time to integrate the meditation with everyday reality.

The ovaries are your creative power, not only to make babies, but it also is the creative power for your projects in the world. This is where the spark of all life begins in a woman! Own your own creative power!

## BLACK MADONNA HEALING BATH MEDITATION

I found that some of my best meditations happen in the bathtub. If you have a busy life or a family the bathroom can become a place of retreat to slip into a sacred space for yourself.

What is needed:
Picture of the Black Madonna of Czechoslovakia
Seven White Carnations
Two cups of Epsom Salt
One cup of natural sea salt
One essential oil (optional)
One candle (Pink or white)
60 minutes to yourself

Pour yourself a hot bath. Take seven white carnations, break up the petals and add them into the bath water. Also add 2 cups of Epsom salt and one cup of natural sea salt. You also might like to add one of your own favorite pure essential oils. My suggestions for essential oils would be one of the following:

Sage oil, for purification
Rose oil, for healing the heart
Clarity Sage. for balancing hormones
Cypress, for transformation

White carnations have jagged edges. Anger viewed on the astral planes also has sharp, jagged edges. As you bathe and meditate, the anger stored in the body will release and be removed as it blends with the carnation petals. Two likes cancel each other out—this is a very simple form of flower essence medicine.

The meditation: Light a candle. Place the picture of the Black Madonna by your candle so you can see her clearly. Turn the lights off, lock the door and slip into the tub. Close your eyes and just let your muscles begin to relax

Begin to breathe full, deep breaths all the way into your belly. Watch your mind begin to slow down. Stare at the Madonna's picture for a while, studying all the details. Remember what she looks like. Now visualize yourself as the Black Madonna. Close your eyes and see your face as the Madonna's face, deep brown skin like the rich soil of the Mother Earth. Picture your eyes as her eyes, all-knowing, fully seeing, yet ever forgiving. It is very important at this part of the meditation that you fully embody the visualization. It does take practice. Now see the scar that goes across her face. You look deeply into the scar and you see that it is filled with golden light. The scar is now glowing and it opens up. Once the scar is open begin to bring forth the wounds that you have suffered as a woman. Take the time to search and admit to yourself where you are suffering. Find one suffering situation and picture all the details and let all the feelings arise. Once this is fully visualized put it into the open golden scar of the Madonna that you are embodying. As you place it into the scar, say the words, "Transformed into Light".

Now conjure another memory of suffering. Fully visualize it. Feel the unresolved feelings and again place it into the golden glowing scar, saying the words, "Transformed into Light".

Just keep repeating the old memories that need to be healed, and each time asking for the Transformation into the Light as you place it into the scar.

You may become weary when you bring forth to many memories that your body and mind may still be holding, so a little bit at a time may be better medicine for new meditators until you become strong enough to face each wound.

If anger arises release it with your breath and let the flowers soothe the emotional wounds that your body has carried. Be gentle with yourself. Do not judge yourself harshly.

If guilt arises know that guilt is the glue that keeps old memories and relationships stuck, release your guilt and release people that are connected to your guilt.

Witnessing the memories can be very helpful during this process. Look at your life as if you are watching a movie on a screen. It helps to see the situation more clearly.

Just keep breathing. Release the memories into the scar and ask for transformation.

When you feel you have had enough make a prayer to the Black Madonna. Ask that your life, heart and womb be healed. Ask for her blessings of transformation. Close up the glowing scar and visualize that the Madonna heals all the experiences. Blow out the candle and let the tub drain.

Quietly lie down for a while in your bedroom and integrate your healing.

This can be a very powerful meditation and should be done as a practice. Womb healing is like peeling the different layers of an onion. It is a process, and takes time and practice to be fully realized.

## FORGIVENESS MEDITATION

Usually when I start this process I take an inventory of how many people I have grievances with and make a list. I use an affirmation to begin with to cleanse my emotions and anger I may be holding which keeps me from forgiving. For example:

**The Christ in me forgives the Christ in you.**
**May Christ's love now heal all grievances between us.**

This becomes your mantra. It is nice if you have prayer beads or a rosary to keep count of each mantra. Now visualize one person that you have not forgiven. Place them in your heart and begin to say the mantra. As the mantra begins all your emotional baggage may come up. The emotional baggage will give you a list of reasons why you should not forgive. Let them arise. Even if anger takes place keep repeating the mantra. At first it is like going down a very bumpy road. Your head will throw out all kinds of excuses to hold on to resentments, but keep repeating your mantra. The emotions from your belly will be all stirred up, but keep repeating the mantra. This may take days or weeks and on karmically challenged relationships it can take months. But keep repeating the mantra and visualize the person who you have the grievances with and forgive. The road will get smoother.

The mantra will cleanse your emotions as they arise and you will begin to see with different eyes. For example one man that I was having a very hard time forgiving I saw as a little boy who was wounded. From that angle I was able to forgive him. You will know when you have completely forgiven when the emotional stuff stops coming up and you feel clean. As the emotions begin to arise you may want to stop. Don't. Remind yourself that you are doing this for yourself.

Unforgiving emotions keep you bound to karmic situations from one life to the next. You are setting yourself free. Negative emotions clog the heart just as cholesterol clogs the arteries.

I have done this with a list people as one big practice and I have also done it by honing in on one person with whom I may have stubborn karmic conditions to overcome. I do this practice as long as it takes. Some situations will be resolved in just a couple of meditations. Others may take weeks and even months.

After you have completed your list of people make inventory again. Do it once a year because life is sometimes full of challenging relationships.

**When I speak about forgiveness meditation I am not talking about staying with a person who is abusive, or letting a person abuse you emotionally or physically for the sake of forgiveness. Women at times put up with abusive patterns in relationships because of their own co-dependent nature. As the Dalai Lama once said, " I forgive the Chinese Communists but it doesn't mean I have to have tea with them."**

## GENETIC HEALING MEDITATION

This is a mantra meditation with visualization. I use the mantras of the Divine Mother. What is important here is to choose an emanation of the Mother that you can relate to.

Virgin Mary
Christian
Hail Mary, full of grace, the Lord is with thee.
Blessed art thou amongst women and blessed is the fruit of thy womb, Jesus.
Holy Mary, Mother of God, pray for us now and at the hour of our death.
Amen

Kuan Yin
Chinese
Namo Kuan Shi Yin Pu Sa

Green Tara
Tibetan
Om Tare Tuttare Ture Soha

Durga
Hindu
(Protective and Wrathful)
Om Dhum Durgayei Namah

I use the word sin is this version of the meditation. The original meaning of the word was used in archery. When you shoot an arrow and do not hit your mark it was called to sin, in other words you are off your center.

Once you choose and learn your mantra pick up your prayer beads and begin to recite the mantra 10 times, then stop. Now visualize your child on the altar of your heart and if you do not have children visualize the image of your own inner child. Ask that all negative patterns that have been carried in the bloodline completely be removed. Now do ten Divine Mother Mantras.

Next put your own Mother on the altar of your heart and ask any sins that she may have committed in her lifetime to be completely forgiven. Then do ten mantras.

Now bring your Mother's mother to the altar of your heart. Ask again for complete forgiveness of all sins committed. Do another ten mantras. Do this also with your Great Grandmother and Great Great Grandmother. It is important to include your Grandfather and Great Grandfathers. Just work through your family tree. Ask for healing for each branch. It helps if you know their names if you don't just say Great Grandmother and so forth.

When you have gone through your Mother's lineage do the same with your Father's Lineage. If you are praying for your own children include each child and also the lineage of their father. This meditation takes time but it is well worth the effort. When you have completed the meditation see the mantra written in golden light running through your blood stream. Thank the Divine Mother for her healing and mercy. Thank your ancestors also.

This meditation I did as I walked to work for about 6 months. It was a time in my life that I was a full time working mother. The only time I had for prayer was when I was walking to work. Many inner realizations were revealed about family patterns during this time. A tremendous liberation for the ancestors can occur when you do this practice.

I returned to this practice with the birth of my first grandchild. I practiced this technique throughout the pregnancy of my daughter-in-law. If you seriously want to heal the patterns of your family you will find the time and the dedication to do the **Great Work.**

## INVOCATIONS

Invocations are an invitation for the Divine to come fully into one's body. It is different from prayer. Prayer is directed to a deity outside yourself. Invocation actually creates the possibility of you becoming the deity. It is extremely important not to identify with becoming the deity. Once the ego attaches itself to this process of merging with the deity you are off track. The deity is only the form of the Divine. The Divine is beyond form or identification with form. The different deities, angels or saints are like stained glass windows through which the light can shine.

You may use Buddhas, Self-Realized Saints or Arch Angels in your invocations. However, never use guides or spirits that have not fully achieved spiritual realization. You may open yourself up to influences that are undesired. Each Buddha or Saint has his/her own office that needs to be applied to in your invocation request. For example, if you need healing you request the Medicine Buddha or Raphael, the Angel or Healing. If you need protection, you call Archangel Michael or the Warrior Buddhas.

Traditionally, Buddhism does not call a woman a Buddha. The females are usually titled Bodhisattvas. However, in my own invocation practice, before I ever knew the difference, I had always addressed the Female Buddhas. They showed up in spite of my ignorance.

This is a very simple form of Tantra that has been translated into a western formula. It is easy to use and can be applied to various situations. The proof is always in the practice. The discipline of daily calling forth is required to obtain real results.

The Western Formula:

**I call forth the Power and the Presence of** _____
*(this part of the invocation is the invitation to the particular deity)*

**I give you my body heart and soul** *(this is the invitation for the deity* *to fully enter your body. It is only through opening the door of your heart that the Enlightened Ones come. You have to actively give permission.)*

Once you have strongly invoked the Presence of the Enlightened One you state your request according to the their particular office. This should be said in your own words from the heart.

# THE ENLIGHTENED ONES

### Female Buddhas Who Never Were Recognized

You may address a Female Buddha in times when you need a wise woman to counsel you. Imagine how many women over time gained enlightenment and left this world without a trace of recognition. I have found they are very happy to be helpful.

### Medicine Buddhas

They can be addressed for any type of healing, both physical, mental or emotional.

### Tantric Buddhas

The Tantric Buddhas know all the secrets of sexual healing and sexual Tantra. They can be invoked before lovemaking to create sacred sexuality.

### The Bodhisattvas

Bodhisattvas are those Enlightened Ones that have vowed to alleviate suffering. When you need an answer to overcome suffering you may be experiencing, you should call the Bodhisattvas.

### Warrior Buddhas

Do not be afraid when they show up because they come with fierce presence and fiery faces. It is through their fierceness that they protect.

### Christ and Mary Magdalene

This Divine Couple can be invoked to heal the separation of spirit and sexuality that Christian negative programming has created in our mental, emotional, and physical bodies. This is a very powerful way to heal the separation. However, one must ask.

### Black Madonna

The dark aspect of the Divine Mother can be invoked for situations that involve sex, death or childbirth.

### Saint Francis of Assisi

I have found miracles have happened to me by invoking Saint Francis. He is the Saint for the protection and healing of animals. He also has been recognized for the Blessings he brings to nature.

### Shiva and Parvati

This Divine Tantric Couple can also be invoked to reveal the sexual secrets of Tantra during lovemaking.

### Maha Lakshmi

The Hindu Goddess of wealth and beauty can be invoked for business ventures or creative endeavors that involve beauty.

### Maha Durga

A wrathful aspect of the Hindu Goddess can be invoked for protection against all forms of evil.

### Saraswati

The Hindu Goddess of education, music, arts and writing can bring her blessings to all your projects.

### Ganesh

The Hindu Elephant God of removing obstacles can be invoked to remove obstacles of all kinds.

*I have found that using mantras of the Hindu Deities with the invocations can be a very powerful form of practice. To learn more about mantras I suggest the book Healing Mantras by Thomas Ashley-Farrand*

## ARCHANGELS

**Archangel Raphael**
He is the angel of healing.
**Archangel Michael**
He is the angel for protection and banishing evil.
**Archangel Gabriel**
Invoke him in situations that need revelation of truth or clarity of communication.
**Archangel Uriel**
This angel holds each soul's record in his hands. Call him to access past lifetimes or karmic information.

There exist many more enlightened ones beyond the above list but this will give you an idea of where to start.

**I also want to give credit to Andreas Mamet for creating and teaching me the invocational formulas. My deepest gratitude goes to him.**

## TANTRIC HEALING

There are many good books on the market today teaching different forms of sexual Tantra. I have found through my own experience that adding prayer and invocation before and during the sexual act can propel a couple beyond theory into direct experience of what Tantra truly is.

Calling the Tantric Buddhas before lovemaking can unlock sexual secrets within the couple.

### Meditation

Bathing each other before Tantra honors the body and prepares a couple for this meditation.

Both partners are nude.

**Invocation: I call forth the Tantric Buddhas. I give you my body, heart and soul. Unfold in the NOW.**

The male and female sit cross-legged, facing each other. You may hold hands, crossing your arms. This creates a figure eight, *the symbol for eternity.*

Now the male should begin to gaze into the left eye of the female. The female in return also gazes into the left eye of the male. Both partners slowly breathe together and watch the rise and fall of theirs breaths. The breathing should go deep into the belly. After a few minutes you will find that you are both breathing together as one. When this happens it is time to invoke out loud. Say:

**I call forth the Tantric Buddhas. I give you our bodies, hearts and souls. Bless us with the secrets of sacred sexuality. Heal our bodies, hearts and souls.**

After repeating the above invocation several times you will begin to feel the Presence of the Buddhas with you. This takes practice. The more you call the quicker the response of the Holy Ones.

Once you feel the Power of the Buddhas you can add your own

request for sexual healing. Create the invocation to fit your own circumstances. If there are issues that concern you address them. You can also ask for the remnants of old relationship patterns to be removed so love and trust can blossom.

Healing Tantra happens in the soil of LOVE and TRUST. This can be a beautiful gift to your beloved and to yourself.

I have found that once the Tantric Buddhas arrive anything is possible during the lovemaking. You can explore together and proceed as you wish.

Once the Love Making is complete remember to seal each Chakra by laying your hand over your beloved. Start with the Crown Chakra by saying:

**May you be sealed and protected by the Tantric Buddhas.**

Now move your hand to the Third Eye Chakra located between the eyebrows and say again:

**May you be sealed and protected by the Tantric Buddhas.**

Do the same with the Chakras of the throat, the heart, and the solar plexus. Finally cup the hand gently over the sexual opening of the woman or the scrotum of the man. Each time you repeat the above invocation.

It also important after lovemaking to take the time to just quietly be with each other. Allow the Tantric energy be fully absorbed into each other's bodies.

# REFERENCES

Books and tools that have helped me along the way
**Woman of Power and Grace**
By Timothy Conway, PHD
Wake Up Press
**The Art of Sexual Ecstasy**
By Margo Anand
Putnam Publishing Group
**The Woman's Encyclopedia of Myths and Secrets**
By Barbara G. Walker,
Harper and Collins Inc. Publishers
**Sexual Secrets**
By Nik Douglas and Penny Slinger
Destiny Books
**The Tao of Love and Sex:**
**The Ancient Chinese Way of Ecstasy**
Jolan Chang
Dutton Paperback
**Healing Mantras**
By Thomas Ashley-Farrand
Ballantine Wellspring paperback
He also has CDs.
**Goddess Symbols**
By Clare Gibson
Barnes and Noble Books
**The Everyday Meditator**
By Osho
Charles E. Tuttle Company, Inc.
**Sacred Woman**
By Queen Afua
Ballantine Books

**The Art of the Bath**
By Sara Slavin and Karl Petzke
Chronicle Books
**Kundalini, the Arousal of Inner Energy**
By Ajit Mookerjee
Destiny Books
**The Encyclopedia of Eastern Philosophy and Religion**
Shambhala Books
**Love Magic**
By Marina Medici
Fireside Simon and Schuster
**The Book of Buddhas**
By Eva Rudy Jansen
Binkey Kok Publication Holland
**The Book of Hindu Imagery**
By Eva Jansen
Binkey Kok Publication Holland
**A Garden of Woman's Wisdom**
By Raylene Veltri, now Raylene Abbott
Halo Books
**Mantra CDs for learning**
**The CDs Mantras 2 to Change the World, Mantras Magical Songs of**
**Power and Mantras 3: A Little Bit of Heaven**
By Henry Marshall and Playshop Family
**The CDs Embrace, The Essence and Love is Space**
By Deva Premal
**Om Namo Narayanaya**
**Chants for Peace**
By Sahadev and Dawn
www.BlueskiesUnlimited.com